About the author

Erling Kagge (Norway) is a ~~p~~.... lawyer, publisher and philosopher. He was the first person in the world to walk alone to the South Pole and to surmount the 'three poles'—North, South and the summit of Mount Everest. Currently, he is also a successful entrepreneur in Oslo-based publishing house Kagge Forlag, and a keen collector of contemporary art. Astrup Fearnley Museum for Modern Art in Oslo exhibited a selection of his collection in 2015.

About the photographer

Steve Duncan is an urban historian, explorer and photographer based in New York City. He has logged more than fifteen years exploring subways, sewers and storm drains around the world. He has ventured through infrastructures beneath Paris, London, Berlin, Los Angeles, and many other cities. Duncan has been very involved in attempting to map out the relationship between historic, natural waterways and the modern sewer and drainage systems in cities today to show how this invisible infrastructure affects the city above.

About the translator

Becky L. Crook studied Linguistics at Seattle Pacific University. In 2008, she moved to Berlin and founded the biannual literary journal, *SAND*. Moving to Delft in 2012, she began to focus on literary translations from the Norwegian and German into English. In 2015, her family relocated to the U.S., where she was granted a writing residency toward her first novel. She enjoys island life and frequently spots orcas near Seattle.

Under Manhattan

Erling Kagge

Under Manhattan

FIVE DAYS BENEATH THE STREETS OF NEW YORK

Translated from the Norwegian
by Becky L. Crook

World Editions

Published in Great Britain in 2015 by World Editions Ltd., London

www.worldeditions.org

Copyright © Erling Kagge, 2012
English translation copyright © Becky L. Crook, 2015
Cover design Multitude
Image credit © Lars Myhren Holand
Images: All of the photographs in the book were taken by Steve Duncan,
with the exception of pp. 16-17, 53, 115, 156-157, 168 (taken by Erling Kagge);
pp. 86-87, 96-97, 124-125, 176-177, 183 (taken by Andrew Wonder);
pp. 170-171 (Stephen Chung/Shutterstock);
pp. 192-193 (taken by Børge Ousland)

First published as *Under Manhattan: en reise til New Yorks indre* in
Norway in 2012 by Kagge Forlag, Norway. Published by agreement with
Leopard förlag, Stockholm and Leonhardt & Høier Literary Agency A/S,
Copenhagen.

British Library Cataloguing-in-Publication Data
A catalogue record for this book is available on request from
the British Library

ISBN 978-94-6238-017-2

Typeset in Minion Pro and Calibri

This translation has been published with the financial support of NORLA

Distribution Europe (except the Netherlands and Belgium):
Turnaround Publisher Services, London
Distribution the Netherlands and Belgium: Centraal Boekhuis,
Culemborg, the Netherlands

To Ingrid, Solveig and Nor

'Does not man, perhaps, love something besides well-being?
[...] Which is better—cheap happiness or exalted suffering?'

Fyodor Dostoyevsky, *Notes from the Underground*

CONTENTS

FRIDAY NIGHT, DECEMBER 17ᵀᴴ, 2010

We extracted waders from our backpacks. The air was chilly and we shivered, but I knew it would be warmer below in the sewers, so I removed my wool sweater before pulling on the pants. I was going to disappear from the earth's surface once again. That was what it felt like. Steve and I perused our surroundings. We were sitting on the stairs outside an exclusive fashion boutique in SoHo, a neighborhood upwards of Canal Street, on the corner of Greene and Grand Streets. Several manhole covers dotted the street ahead of us, all embossed in iron with *NYC Sewer Made in India*. We'd tried opening many of them, to no avail. As we squatted in the street, coaxing, struggling, and attempting to pry them loose, a few cars motored past and some passers-by walked down along Greene. One couple looked like they'd just come out of a bar. A hipster with a miniature moustache seemed to be on his way to work. Unwilling to risk discovery, we passed the time on the steps below the fashion boutique, waiting. Finally, the street was still. We jumped up and sprinted to another manhole, each stood on one side of it, inserted our fingers down into the holes and heaved up. It gave way. We pushed the cover to the side. It was one of the smaller models, easy to lift. Steve climbed down first and I followed suit. It was now 3.32 a.m. on Friday, December 17th.

Once I was down in the hole, I slid the cover back over my head. It clanked into place. Suddenly pitch-blackness surrounded us. Five or six feet below, I could hear the sewer babbling. I pulled my flashlight out of a pouch on my belt, switched it on, and continued my descent. The shaft going down was narrow. Steve was waiting for me at the bottom. The tunnel hardly afforded space for two people. It was constructed of concrete, nearly three feet high and just about as wide. The temperature was several degrees warmer due to the sewage, the air was dense, and the stench pungent. Bending forward, Steve disappeared ahead of me on his way toward Canal Street. He had dreamed of discovering this part of the city for a long time. I switched on the air gauge fastened to my right breast pocket. It measured zero for poisonous gases and 20.9 for oxygen. Perfect conditions. I crouched down and began the trek forward, knees bent, back hunched, and arms out in front so as to make my body as small as possible. It was hard going and I had trouble breathing. We moved slowly. The stream of sewage flowed in the direction we were heading. At this late hour of the night, more grey water is flushed down than toilet emissions. 'It's a nice time of day to be navigating the sewers,' called Steve.

The trickle and rush of sewage was an ever-present sound. Added to that was the rumbling of traffic above, along Greene. Each time a car wheel hit a manhole cover, there was a loud clang. The roar of the engine eventually subsided, but the reverberation of the manhole cover continued ringing in the metal overhead.

The closer we came to Canal, the lower and narrower the tunnel became. Peering far ahead, I could see that the tunnel widened out again. Steve called back to me. I couldn't hear exactly

We had already been underway for four days, but it was the first time I found myself asking: What the hell am I doing here?

what he was saying, but I understood his meaning: neither of us had expected the ceiling to be lower than fifteen inches. This wasn't exactly something to ponder at a crouch, however, so I

13

placed my hands on the tunnel floor and inched forward. I soon had to lie flat on my stomach. Wiggling my forearms and knees, I squirmed forward on all fours. The sewer pipes are periodically filled with muck and water. When the water level sinks again, chunks of excrement are left dangling from the top, along with garlands of toilet paper. Our challenge was to elevate our bodies above the floor while simultaneously avoiding contact with the tunnel's ceiling. But it was too tight. Above ground, the air was dry and brisk, but down here it was muggy, and the warm steam from the sewage wafted into our faces. The stench burned in my nose. I continued my forward scrabble, the filth alternately skimming my chest and my back. My gloves were sopping, and after a few more feet, my hat and jacket were also smeared with muck.

I should, of course, have brought along waterproof gloves, but it was too late now, and up to this point it'd all gone well. I worried a bit about infections. I'd contracted several small scratches from the previous days' sewer excursions, clambering around between barbed wire and rough concrete. A few more feet ahead and I could no longer avoid the sewage: both my chest and my back pressed against the roof and floor of the tunnel.

A brown rat, a *Rattus norvegicus*, inspected me from a few feet away, along the sewage rim. Our heads were level above the waste. I looked into two curious eyes. It didn't blink. Charles Darwin determined that both the rat and I belonged to the animal kingdom, but beyond that, no one had shown what other subjective experiences we might share, except for sight and sound. But neither the sight of me covered in muck nor the sound of me grunting from exhaustion seemed to faze the rodent.

Down there, with the rat, I observed myself as if from a bird's-eye perspective. 'Life is like a sewer, [...] what you get out of it depends on what you put in.' This is life wisdom from mathematics professor and artist Tom Lehrer. I found myself in a funny kind of situation. The rat finally darted off. I looked further into the tunnel. What else was hiding down there? We had already been underway for four days, but it was the first time I found myself asking: What the hell am I doing here?

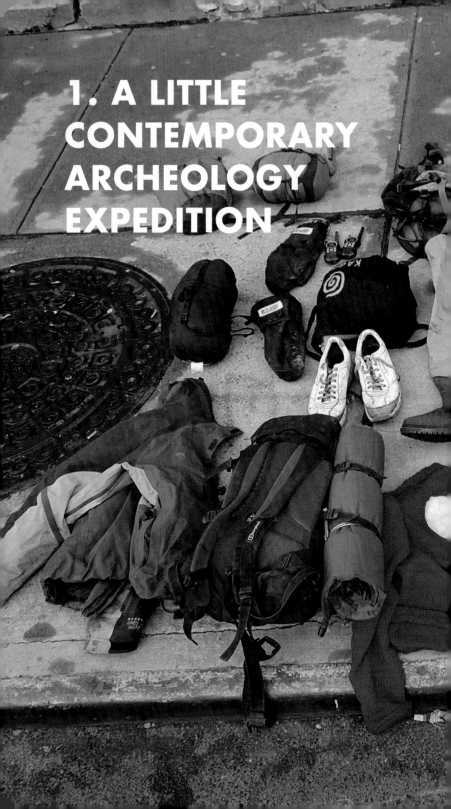

1. A LITTLE CONTEMPORARY ARCHEOLOGY EXPEDITION

All of us are born explorers.

You, me, and everyone else.

Exploration is what propels us forward in our first years. When my three daughters were young, they climbed on chairs, up stairs, and up hillsides before they had even learned to walk. But as soon as they started walking upright, moving around on two legs, they stopped climbing.

An explorer is not something that we become, it's what we are. A child wonders intuitively what is hidden beyond the next ridge. It wants to discover more space around itself. This is our natural state. The joy and curiosity is there from day one, but it often disappears gradually as we grow older. Parents, schools, friends, and employers all have their own expectations of and ideas about how a young person should develop and act, and these expectations come at the cost of our exploratory nature. This is the price of civilization. I have given in to this many times myself, and have also taught my children to do the same. Every nation is founded on the idea that the majority of its inhabitants should contribute to the gross national product. I work, produce children, and pay taxes. There shouldn't be too many people who opt out of this system.

This wasn't the first time I'd travelled far toward a singular goal, searching for meaning in life. I had sailed to West Africa, pursued the sun across the Atlantic Ocean, through the Panama Canal, and to the Galapagos, heading further through the Pacific Ocean to Antarctica, around Cape Horn, and to the Falkland Islands, and from the Caribbean back to Norway. To the world's outer edges. Together with Børge Ousland and Geir Randby, I cross-country skied from Ellesmere Island, Canada to the North Pole. Just after this expedition, I decided to go in the opposite direction. I wanted to be the first person to ski alone to the South Pole. By the time I arrived at that pole after fifty days, without having seen or spoken to another person, I'd already decided to be the first person to reach all three of the earth's extremes: the North Pole, the South Pole, and Mount Everest. A little more than a year later, I stood atop the world's tallest mountain.

An explorer is not something that we become, it's what we are. A child wonders intuitively what is hidden beyond the next ridge. It wants to discover more space around itself. This is our natural state.

The view from 29,000 feet above sea level was overwhelming. The experience was a valuable one of camaraderie and the pleasure of being in nature. All of the meticulous planning and the struggle to reach the top made it even more worthwhile to finally get there. But the feeling of elation on top of the world's tallest mountain doesn't last very long before you start asking yourself: How in the world am I going to get down from here? How am I going to keep going?

When Roald Amundsen reached the South Pole in 1911, as the first person to do so, his thoughts were in quite another place: I have never been so far from my goal. (Amundsen's dream since boyhood had been to be the first to reach the North Pole.)

Voyages of Discovery

In my experience, happiness is something that I might come across anywhere, at any time, and even in totally unexpected ways. For me, happiness is rarely a state of mind. When I'm on an expedition, it could be the warmth returning to my body, or when I'm full after eating, or when a good thought surfaces. But the cold, the struggle, and the sweat also serve to remind me how difficult it is to understand what it is that I actually want. Pain and uncertainty go hand in hand with the joy of being on your own voyage of discovery.

Classical voyages of discovery—or perhaps *re*discovery, which most of them actually were, since there were always people standing on beaches, observing newcomers like Columbus, Cook, Magellan and Erikson as they 'discovered' the new worlds—are about travelling as far as possible from your starting point. Outward, forward, and maybe even upward. With the purpose of uncovering something that heretofore was just a blank space on a map.

So one day I flipped my usual ambitions on their head. Turn it around, I thought. Don't travel in a single direction, or up and out. This time, stop, head downward, go underground where the sun never shines. Find your own way. Experience freedom by escaping from the daily grind. Look for happiness and joy where not many people have thought to look before.

I wanted to see myself from another perspective and to get to know New York more intimately by discovering its sewers, viewing its structures from below. To disappear down into the shadows, so that each time I resurfaced I would take in the billboards, the din, and follow the bustle of Christmas preparations. From north in the Bronx to Manhattan, through Brooklyn and Queens and out to the Atlantic, part native and part explorer, underground in what I imagined to myself as the city's subconscious. That part of the city that no one considers as long as water flows from the tap, foundations stand solid, waste vanishes down toilets, and subways follow their routes, but which is essential for the life that takes place above ground. I wanted to experience how this city, which I like more than any other, appears from below, with a perspective shifted by 180 degrees. What's down there? What is New York like inside out? Is there a system? Does anyone live down there, in the belly of the city?

And could I start to understand those things I'd encounter on my journey by revisiting Aristotle, listening to Lady Gaga, and reading Dante Alighieri's classical work *The Divine Comedy*, about his sojourn through the underworld?

I had good reasons for bringing Dante along on my trip. Dante's journey also begins when he is halfway through his life. He realizes he is lost. Together with his companion and guide, Virgil, Dante travels through the abyss and further on, through purgatory and paradise—the two really undertook some serious existential travel. At the very beginning of the tale, there's a scene I can't forget. Dante imagines himself as a drowning man. He pulls through by the skin of his teeth, but as his feet finally reach solid ground and he sits gasping for breath he does not look on ahead, but rather backward, toward the direction from which he came—toward the sea and the unpredictability that he'd just escaped. As I sat reading the scene, I could very well recognize the feeling. Life can sometimes seem too safe and predictable—your comfort zone can become your world. So I was long on safety and coziness, but as befalls most men at some point in the middle of their lives, I was desperate to leave it all behind. I felt a gnawing restlessness and turmoil throughout my whole body, and I wanted to feel present in my own life again.

Many of my expeditions have taken place in pristine, clean and sunny environments. The white expanses of the poles, the vast blue, glittering oceans and Everest, getting closer to the sun than I had ever been. Now I wanted to descend into the dark, man-made dungeons of New York.

My site was not chosen at random. The city has always been good to me. I've fallen in love there, seen the best art, formed lasting friendships, and indulged in every way. New York has given me highs of all kinds.

It is the city of all modern cities. That small, compact island of Manhattan sprouts continually upward, never outward, to accommodate its many inhabitants, and it also houses a little-known, man-made wilderness beneath its surface. Of course New York rarely scores high on lifestyle surveys. The air quality isn't the best, everything is expensive, social inequality is vast, and space is limited. Yet despite all of that, I get the impression that it's the place people most want to live. Preferably right smack in the middle of Manhattan even beneath it.

Steve Duncan

My original intention was to go solo. But then I read about the American Steve Duncan, aged 32, and his trips beneath the city. His experiences would undoubtedly make the journey both safer and more interesting. Steve is a legend among a small group of urban explorers: people who go around discovering the cityscape and its man-made reality. I called him up and we agreed to meet some months later, in August 2010. I flew to New York and we walked for sixty blocks under Manhattan. The trip took most of a Saturday.

I told him about my idea: to cross New York through a network of tunnels in different neighborhoods. The plan would be to navigate from the deep innards of the city, through sewage, water runoff, garbage, and confined air, out toward the salty water of the ocean. Since the tunnel systems were not always connected, we would occasionally have to surface and continue above ground.

Steve had never heard of anything like this, and he accepted at once. His dreams of rediscovering the city's subterranean history had taken root during his earlier studies at Columbia University. According to Steve, exploring the underground is akin to opening a clock and examining all the gears and mechanisms that make it tick.

According to Steve, exploring the underground is akin to opening a clock and examining all the gears and mechanisms that make it tick.

Steve's dream began like this: one evening he couldn't get into the mathematics building. The doors were locked and he'd been out too late. Finally giving up, Steve asked another student if there were any alternative entrances. The student said yes, and pointed, instructing: 'Go in that direction and you'll come to the main tunnel. Take that, and follow the steam pipes.' Steve followed the student's tip, but first he just stood peering into the university's unlit tunnels. Should he go in? He had always been afraid of the dark and had to struggle with himself to face the inky blackness. 'If I were able to go into the tunnel and further on into the dark,' he thought to himself, 'I'd have something to really be proud of.' Thus began Steve's deep interest in life underground, or, as he calls it, each city's microcosmos. After that incident, he switched majors and began studying Urban History, but he thought it was more exciting to observe the course of history with his own eyes and to be able to touch with two hands what he was studying.

Steve has decided to use the next years to inform the outside world about what he's found hidden below the city's streets.

'I love the idea—though I'm not alone in this—to be one of those people who knows the city's ancient maps,' Steve told me in his laid-back Maryland accent, 'and to be someone who has really been there and has really experienced it, until one day I can say, like Robert Frost, that I "knew the brook, its strength / And impulse, having dipped a finger length / And made it leap my knuckle."'

I prefer to travel alone or in a small group. This is the Norwegian ideal, but this was New York. As our December trip drew near, I quickly began to understand that it would be different. On some parts of our journey, Steve and I would travel alone, but we would have company on other portions. A *New York Times* reporter, Alan Feuer, had heard about the trip from his boss a few days before we were to start. 'Alan, listen,' his boss said. 'A Norwegian explorer and another guy are planning an expedition through the underground. I thought of you immediately. You interested?' Alan accepted immediately. He said it was like getting an assignment for a wilderness-exploration party from the nineteenth or early twentieth century dropped in his lap. Also, Jacki Lyden from *NPR* was going to make a radio program about the trip, and Brent Baughman would accompany her to record sound.

Andrew Wonder, Liz Rush, and Will Hunt are all urban explorers and also wanted in. Andrew is a photographer and planned to film parts of our journey. Liz is Steve's girlfriend. For their first date, Steve took her to the top of Manhattan Bridge—a slick move that apparently worked. She later told me: 'When we reached the top, twilight was falling, and I knew this was the start of something—I fell in love with both Steve and the amazing city.'

Will Hunt was writing a book on urban exploration. In his

brown horn-rimmed glasses and elegant scarf, he looked more like he was on his way to a café. He had a penchant for philosophy, too: 'I've always thought that guys like Steve view the city the way a surgeon views a human body: with a single piercing

---

Everyday life is sometimes short of one of life's most vital emotions: excitement. 'I know of an Englishman,' wrote Johan Wolfgang von Goethe on one occasion, 'who hanged himself so he wouldn't have to knot his tie every morning.'

---

glance, they've mastered the city's anatomy. For them, the physical environment is a kind of photographic negative of itself. The city's surface is stripped away, and that which was suppressed and marginalized comes to light.'

Steve assured me that he and I would be the only ones to complete the whole trip. For me, the two of us were the primary explorers on the trip. I paid little attention to the others who came and went. 'The others are going to psych themselves out,' Steve said to me. He wasn't putting anyone down, he was just predicting that no one else would want to go the whole way. The next days would prove him right.

The Cycle of Civilization

Everyday life is sometimes short of one of life's most vital emotions: excitement. 'I know of an Englishman,' wrote Johan Wolfgang von Goethe on one occasion, 'who hanged himself so he wouldn't have to knot his tie every morning.' Though I've never been that extreme, there are times when each day seems to blend in with all the rest. Hope, love, joy, and anger seem to flatten out when life becomes habitual. Excitement is absent. The days are all the same. The challenge— assuming an average Norwegian life expectancy—is that I have about 30,000 days to seek my own path. And at this moment, being fortunate enough to have about 12,000 days left, I've already long since learned that the greatest luxuries in life are time and good health.

Steve and I continued planning our little contemporary archeology expedition during the fall of 2010. I like making preparations. It's exciting. Travelling is like falling in love, and can be almost all-consuming. We decided we would start the trip on Monday, December 13th, 2010, at Van Cortlandt Park and 242nd Street in the north part of the city, and then walk south through the sewage system beneath the Bronx, down beneath Broadway toward Harlem. We chose the date for two reasons: that's when Steve would be finished with his semester, and I wanted to see New York decorated for Christmas each time I popped up out of the sewer.

I enjoyed imagining the contrast between the plain, dingy atmosphere under the city and the lively, circus-like bustle up above. Within the space of a few hours, we would experience an entire cycle of civilization. Above ground there would be lavish party preparations, hectic Christmas shopping, and restaurants bursting with parched and famished guests, while just below, the end product of civilization—forgotten bits of trash and excrement—would be streaming past. It was a cycle we hoped to experience first-hand.

On Packing a Bag

The art of packing a bag for an expedition is about knowing the difference between those things that one absolutely *must* bring and those things that one might just prefer to take along. It's the battle between need-to-have and nice-to-have, where need-to-have always wins. The future and the past are also of little importance on an expedition. Old habits should be left at home. Underway, one's thoughts are confined to the joys and dangers of the journey; these consume all your attention.

We didn't determine ahead of time how many days the trip should take, or exactly which routes we would follow. Our backpacks contained everything that Steve and I would need: sleeping bags, thin air mattresses, warm jackets, tools for opening and marking the manhole covers, air gauges, wading pants, and a small stove and pan apiece.

It's always a good feeling, a liberating feeling, to carry everything I need on my back. I can eat and sleep wherever I want, whenever I want, and I'm not dependent on anyone else.

2. VAN CORTLANDT PARK, 242ND STREET, BRONX: NORTH OF THE NORTH POLE

As a lawyer, I would probably start this chapter with a disclaimer discouraging people from trying something like this themselves. But as an explorer, I say, go ahead!

A good rule of thumb for those who plan to walk and crawl around in sewage pipes is to have an idea how you can get back up before you climb down. It can take a while to find the perfect manhole. In large cities there are countless manholes, though this fact had previously escaped my attention. The real challenge, though, is that they all look alike from down in the sewer, even by the light of a head lamp: a narrow, grime-covered ladder, usually rusty, ascending through a small shaft of stone or brick, and, settled on top, a dirty, grey, circular cast-iron closure. Manholes are often in the middle of the street. Along Broadway—the enormous street that stretches nearly the entire length of New York, and which we planned to follow through the Bronx—the unending traffic made it impossible to attempt opening one of the hatches. The risk was too great for getting a tire in the head or incurring gruesome injuries.

'You cannot travel the path until you have become the path itself,' stated Buddha. After several weeks on my fifty-day walk to the South Pole, completely alone with myself and the frozen landscape, I began to feel as though I were part of it. The surroundings and the weather became an extension of myself. 'Here, I can hear and enjoy the silence, and it feels good to be alone in the world,' I wrote in my journal on the fourteenth day, amid the endless white of snow and ice. As the landscape around me and the landscape between my ears melded, I could sense a deep peace. Eight days later, on day twenty-two, I continued writing:

'At home, I only seem to appreciate "big bites." Being down here teaches me to value small pleasures—a nuance in the color of the snow, the wind as it lays itself to rest, a warm drink, the patterns of the cloud formations. The stillness.' I had become part of Buddha's proverbial path.

Rushing is the opposite of exploring. Stress rarely engenders happiness, nor does it lead to surprises. It can certainly be essential at times in achieving one's goals, but stress stirs up the feeling that one is living on autopilot: I perform and act, but hardly ever reflect on what I am doing. In New York, it was a challenge for me to avoid stress, even when I found myself underground. When you're wading through slick excrement, clambering over barbed wire, avoiding being hit by an impending train or subway in the dark or a car that might come barreling past at the very moment you open the manhole cover, there's a lot to think about. All this on top of preferably having a good time. Following Buddha's idea of immersion into one's surroundings is, I found, essential to achieving this aim.

The Nice Thing about Freezing

There are several manhole covers in the asphalt along Exterior Street, a small side street stretching south from 230th Street and Broadway. We ambled down Exterior, sometimes on the paved sidewalk, sometimes in the street. We were on the lookout for a suitable manhole that we might exit from later. Tall brownstones built as public housing defined the area. The buildings were owned by the city. Several parking lots were enclosed by barbed wire, and further down the street we could see an auto-repair shop. It was dark; only the street lamps shed a few pale beams onto the street. It was snowing. And it was chilly, maybe below freezing and with an additional gust of wind. In a way, it's easier to keep warm in the middle of Antarctica than it is in New York on a cold night. When you're in the city, you move around much less, the damp air is rawer, and you tend to dress inadequately. In New York, the wind barrels down through the streets, creating wind tunnels between the tall buildings—particularly in Manhattan, with its grid system and almost completely symmetrical road network. If a blast of wind sweeps down a street, there is little to stand in its way. I took off my pants on the street corner, dug a pair of long underwear out of my backpack, and pulled them on. Jacki had a good laugh as I stood on the pavement with bare legs and feet, but it was just something that had to be done. The nice thing about freezing is that it feels so good to warm up again afterwards. I knew it would be warmer in the sewers, but we were still some hours away from our descent.

Each time a car passed, we had to act like we were busy with something else. One of the challenges of manholes in busy streets is that every car that rolls across wedges them further and further in, making them harder to loosen and lift up. They jam quickly and become almost impossible to budge. We went from one to the next, struggling to pry them open with a crowbar. The manhole covers leading to sewers in this part of the Bronx all have the words *BB sewer* stamped clearly on top, making them easy to locate. The first five were stuck tightly, but then we found one that we were able to open. Steve fastened a red thread to the edge and let it dangle to the base of the tunnel below. This was our plan for avoiding confusion as to which hole we should come out of when we—hopefully—returned later that night.

We decided to start the expedition in Van Cortlandt Park, which is located on 242nd Street, directly east of Broadway in the Bronx. From our start, we would follow a water tunnel to the sewage system to begin our journey.

From Ape to Man

The park appeared ill-maintained. Fallen branches and trash lay scattered about. At the park's north end, we could make out a white mansion dating from the time that the Bronx wasn't the Bronx, but a rural, almost untouched area no one had heard of before. For most New Yorkers, 242nd Street is so far north that it might just as well be north of the North Pole.

In Tom Wolfe's novel *The Bonfire of the Vanities*, which is an attempt to define the essence of New York, the Bronx is discussed as the Third World. The main character, a banker and self-designated 'Master of the Universe,' takes a wrong turn from JFK airport to Manhattan and ends up in the Bronx. His lover is in the car with him. Thus begins a very unhappy tale. Nearly paralyzed by the fear of finding themselves in the Bronx, they are forced to stop the car when their way is blocked by a tire. Two black men appear and offer to help. Increasingly desperate, the banker and his lover decide to flee. He pushes the gas pedal to the floor and hits one of the two men, but instead of stopping to check on the man, he opens full throttle and drives away. Later, back at the love nest, his girlfriend praises him for his heroic actions. She credits him for their escape and dubs him 'The King of the Jungle.'

The Bronx also held an exotic fascination for me, but on this night, as so often happens, I discovered that most places are much nicer than people who have never been there before think.

The subway lines along Broadway are elevated one story above street level where they run in the Bronx. The houses are only a few stories high. The subway runs frequently, and rumbles loudly as it passes. I had never been so far north in the city before, and until I had studied the map, I hadn't even been aware that Broadway stretched so far. At the same time, it felt like I'd been here before. Of course: I recognized scenes from car chases in action films, where the heroes, bandits, and policemen pursue one another in frenzied chases, weaving wildly beneath the subway lines, full speed ahead.

It kept snowing. Both Steve and I knew what this could mean. We hardly knew each other but I could tell he was worried. A troubled look crossed his face as we discussed our plans. Outside of urban areas, precipitation is absorbed by the earth, but in New York, soil is almost non-existent. Nature has been usurped, and each hour that it snows increases the danger of cumulative runoff in the sewers. The draining water swells in the constriction of the underground pipes. But the snow would have to melt and become water before it could flood the pipes, so we figured we had a bit of time. We agreed to risk it.

I ambled away from the others and the police car. It wouldn't be good news for any of us to be arrested, but as a foreigner I risked having my US visa revoked. I thought I might be able to melt off into the darkness if the police got too inquisitive.

Arriving at 242nd Street, opposite the yellow-and-red neon signs of Mr. Lee's Chinese Kitchen Taco, we walked briskly toward Van Cortlandt Park. All of the expedition participants had gathered—Jacki, Brent, Will, Andrew, Alan, Steve, and I—with the exception of Liz, who was at home studying for an exam. It was just past midnight and there was no one else in sight. There's so much light in New York that large parks are often the only places from where it's possible to see the stars, but on this evening there was a low cloud cover, so we couldn't see more than a few feet ahead. Now and then our path was lighted up. A number of permanent, rusted barbeque grills were distributed throughout the park. After three hundred feet we heard a car engine and turned. A police car drove toward us. We stopped. 'What's our official story?' someone asked, as the car got closer. We knew we weren't allowed in the park so late at night. 'Say that we're filming a documentary,' said someone else.

We had already nearly been arrested earlier in the day while doing reconnaissance around a bridge and water tunnel at Highbridge Park. There are lots of rules and regulations in New York, and it was our plan to break several of them. No major offences, mind you, but Richard Ford, unfortunately, was right when he wrote: 'Sometimes you have to do the wrong thing just to know you're alive.' A white police car with large NYPD letters across the side pulled up and two uniformed officers peered out at us. One of them rolled down his window. Both grimaced in their short-sleeved shirts as the cold air hit them. 'You're aware that the parks are off-limits at night?' said the one closest to us with a stern expression. I ambled away from the others and the police car. It wouldn't be good news for any of us to be arrested, but as a foreigner I risked having my US visa revoked. I thought I might be able to melt off into the darkness if the police got too inquisitive. According to Steve, the police in New York are not concerned, first and foremost, about well-educated white folks in parks, tunnels, and bridges at night. But if we'd been junkies, dark-skinned, or had been wearing turbans, it might have been a different story.

The officers didn't exactly look like they wanted to get out of their car and into the frigid air to win an argument. That, at least, is one advantage of the cold. Andrew explained that he was a student who had to turn in a completed film project at the New York University the next day. The police officer was silent for a moment. He looked at us and was curt: 'All right, but you gotta wrap it up.' We nodded and hurried into the grove of trees north of the walkway. So far, so good.

You Can't Trust Sewage

We continued without a pathway. At our left, a small bird-preservation area suddenly took me by surprise. I wouldn't have known what it was, had it not been for a tiny, discreet sign providing information about the space. It made me happy, the thought that someone had initiated something like this here in the Bronx.

After walking across uneven terrain we finally arrived at the water. Our way ahead was blocked by a six-foot-tall fence and a gate locked with a chain. On our right was a solitary lamp post with no bulb. It was dark and we wanted to avoid using our flashlights, which might alarm others or attract the police. The fence was easily scaled. On the other side, we headed toward the water's edge. Further on, we stopped at a wall above the water and the tunnel and looked down. In the dim light, we could see that the water level was high. Judging by the sound, large amounts of water were surging through the tunnel below. Steve broke off some branches and attempted to measure the water's depth. It didn't work. I started feeling anxious that we didn't have much time. The police could return at any minute and then it would all be over for the evening. Steve extracted a rope and tied it around his waist. Holding on to the other end, we lowered him down so he could examine the situation.

You can't trust sewage. We knew that a rapid flow twelve to fourteen inches deep would make for difficult walking conditions, and any more flooding could easily cause us to lose our footing. The first sign that a flood wave is coming is silence, followed by a powerful gust of wind through the tunnel just ahead of the surge. The sewage flows into an enormous water-treatment plant, which removes undesirable objects and treats the remaining fluid before it finds its way into the Atlantic Ocean. Being swept like a passive morsel down through a tunnel, with no control over direction or speed, wasn't really part of our plan.

Steve beamed his light toward the shadows, stood and contemplated for a while, and then asked us what we thought. We asked him the same thing. I was not really interested in postponing our departure and waiting for a change in the weather. It could get worse in a few hours. We agreed to make an attempt. Jacki and Brent would stay with Will. Steve had persuaded him to spend the night waiting at the marked manhole in Exterior Street in exchange for coming along with us through a subway tunnel later on. Those of us who remained—Alan, Andrew, and I—dropped our backpacks down to Steve before lowering ourselves into the darkness.

3. THE BRONX SEWERS: PARADISE IS WHERE I AM

I was relieved when I could feel my feet touch the bottom of the tunnel entrance. Finally, we were on our way. 'Abandon all hope, ye who enter here,' read the inscription above the gate to hell in Dante's *Divine Comedy*. But I was more interested in what Dante's guide, Virgil, had to say before they started out: 'Here one must leave behind all doubt; here every cowardice must meet its death.' It was good advice.

I'm always somewhat scared before an expedition begins. I lie awake at night, worrying. But as soon as I take the first steps, the fear releases its hold. It is important, because fear can lead to passivity. Nevertheless, I am always somewhat apprehensive throughout the journey. The feeling is essential for remaining vigilant and alert to danger. Too much self-confidence can lead to mistakes. This trip was no exception.

I shone my flashlight into the tunnel. It was murky and hard to see for more than five or six feet. We walked in and looked around. The beam of my flashlight revealed a world of compost and decay. We were surrounded by everything that society wants to get rid of: dirty water and waste, tampons, and garbage that had been flushed down drainpipes from the thousands of homes above our heads. There's a particular hierarchical structure of topography that is repeated in classical as well as contemporary literature, but especially in film. High up above are the heavens, which we associate with everything good. Deep down below are hell, horror, death, and uncertainty, or else a place where, like Alice in Wonderland, you can slip away and disappear from daily life. The well-illuminated level is ruled by order, predictability, and good weather. At the opposite end is a different weather system, and secrets lie undiscovered. In Bob Dylan's 'Subterranean Homesick Blues,' the underground is the last alternative where one can escape from society's expectations: 'Better jump down a manhole,' sings Dylan, for 'You don't need a weather man/To know which way the wind blows.'

This filthy stream was originally an open river that ran through the Bronx. At the end of the 1800s, the river, Tibbetts Brook, was covered up and routed underground. Slowly but surely, the city took over the wilderness. Today, nature has nearly been supplanted. There's something poetic about all of those city rivers

---

In the sharp gleam of the flashlight, I could see how the tunnel had undergone a refinement process since its construction. Thanks to the countless floods that for more than a century filled the tunnel up to its arched roof in water and waste, the bricks were polished.

---

throughout the world that have been unceremoniously eliminated from the earth's surface and buried below asphalt, rarely to be seen again. I miss them, even if I don't often realize it. The tunnel had scarcely been built with the intention of being beautiful, but it was beautiful nonetheless. A new landscape had been formed for those who were fortunate enough to witness it. The material that was used for construction was red brick, painstakingly laid in a circular pattern 360 degrees around us—walls, floor, and ceiling—everything crafted in the same stone for as far as we could see ahead of us.

In the sharp gleam of the flashlight, I could see how the tunnel had undergone a refinement process since its construction. Thanks to the countless floods that for more than a century filled the tunnel up to its arched roof in water and waste, the bricks were polished. They emitted a soft red glow and were richer in color than other bricks. In addition, they had a soft, pale-golden sheen, a bit like velvet.

When I took up the back of the line, I could see the beams of light from the others in the darkness ahead of me. It was almost like being out fishing on the ocean at night, watching the headlights from fishing boats bobbing in the dark.

We headed south, toward Broadway. As long as we were below the park we mostly waded through water, but as we got close to residential areas and to the sewage pipe that runs along Broadway, the water became a mixture of run-off, soapy water, and garbage.

'We love New York,' I shouted, and we heard the echo ahead in the direction we were heading. The water level wasn't high enough to be worrisome. The snowfall, which could inhibit our itinerary, hadn't melted yet. We walked in pace with the flow. The floor was uneven in places, and I stepped carefully to avoid tripping. I had only brought a few extra pieces of clothing on the trip, so a plunge into the sewer on the first day would have been both impractical and uncomfortable.

Steve was the first to report a leak in his supposedly waterproof waders. Soon after, I also began to feel cold water seeping into my pants. I was soaked. On our climb into the tunnel we had both most likely scraped a couple of holes into our pants. Alan, Steve, Andrew, and I took a small break up on a ledge. Steve said that he was freezing. 'Steve,' I said, 'the water is cold, but remember it will all get warmer as soon as we get into proper sewage.' Steve nodded. He later told me that he appreciated this kind of optimism. There was nothing we could do about the holes in our waders. And so I adhered to my philosophy which states that whatever I can't change, I must, like a good stoic, attempt to accept.

The Root of All Wisdom

The depth of the grimy water varied with the ground surface and with the amount of garbage and other refuse that formed small dams. Sometimes we walked through water that came up to our ankles, at other times it reached our thighs. Andrew's waders barely went up to his thighs. Each time the water level rose, it seeped in. When you find yourself below ground, wandering through sewage, there's not much point in complaining because no one is going to be very interested. So Andrew kept quiet and chuckled at himself.

We took turns going first. Each of us wanted to see as much as possible, and I don't think that any of us was in a hurry to go quickly. When I took up the back of the line, I could see the beams of light from the others in the darkness ahead of me. It was almost like being out fishing on the ocean at night, watching the headlights from fishing boats bobbing in the dark.

I was walking behind Alan when he suddenly slipped and fell on his back. He was sopping wet. That was a little baptism for you, I thought. I didn't know him well and wondered whether he would regret coming with us, now that he was coated in grime.

One of the most common questions people ask me is if I ever have regrets when I'm on an expedition. I try not to expend energy on these kinds of emotions, because it's wasted time. Or, as the Danish philosopher Søren Kierkegaard wrote in his book *Either/Or: A Fragment of Life*, in which the title also constitutes the book's main theme: 'Marry, and you will regret it; don't marry, you will also regret it; [...] laugh at all the world's foolishness or weep over it, you will regret it either way; [...] Believe a woman or believe her not, you will regret it both ways. [...] Hang yourself, you will regret it; do not hang yourself, and you will regret that too; [...] This, gentlemen, is the root of all wisdom.' Alan carefully picked himself up, looked down at the squalid, indeterminate mess that now coated his clothes, shook his head, and smiled.

Negative Beauty

While underground, I had to concentrate to find beauty and worth in my surroundings. Beauty was by no means an absolute in the sewers, but I was determined to look for it, and in this frame of mind I managed to glimpse it emerging now and then.

I have always been most intrigued by expedition narratives in which the descriptions touch on the positive experiences of what *isn't* there. When I read about George Mallory, one of the legendary pioneers of Everest in the 1920s, I understood for the first time the extent to which long journeys have been about just this idea. Mallory and his colleagues didn't go to the Himalayas first and foremost because of what they would find, but rather because of everything that wasn't to be found at those heights: heat, oxygen, predictable weather, and safety. It must have been nearly impossible for those boys to distinguish exhaustion from happiness. The presence of one assumed the other. If climbing Everest had been a cakewalk, they probably wouldn't have bothered, and would have chosen a different mountain.

That's how it was underground in New York. The subterranean wilderness had obviously been designed for functionality and not for aesthetic appeal, but it nonetheless contained its own beauty, which was a negative beauty by virtue of everything that did not exist. A sojourn in this place was not particularly comfortable. It smelled foul, and the air up ahead would only get worse. There was never a quiet moment. We were barraged by noise the entire time, from far away or nearby. There were almost no colors. The

---

The subterranean wilderness had obviously been designed for functionality and not for aesthetic appeal, but it nonetheless contained its own beauty, which was a negative beauty by virtue of everything that did not exist.

---

absence of usual colors such as yellow, blue, or green made it so that I began to distinguish more easily all the variations of brown and grey that dominated our surroundings. The humidity and steam hung like a fog in the tunnel because the air was cooler than the water, which was warmed up by the decomposition of the sewage.

One finds neither peace nor safety in the sewer. You can hardly see just ahead of you. And this is precisely where beauty is to be found—although it's not always easy to see it. 'It's not what you look at that matters, it's what you see,' wrote author, anarchist, and philosopher Henry David Thoreau once. A mountain framed by blue sky is regarded as a thing of beauty, and the same can be said for a symmetrical face, or a painting of cows on a green, flowering meadow. The walk through the sewer offered an opposing view of that which characterizes conventional beauty in everyday life. Despite the fact that nature had been supplanted and had mostly ceased to exist, I was able to view the sewage system below the Bronx as something other than ugly, with the exception of the human excrement, in which I was never quite able to perceive beauty. The architectural structure of pipelines below ground is very much like a living organism: tunnels are built and extended, pathways are rerouted, new building foundations are laid, new pipes are joined to the old, and the underground terrain is altered, all of this without much public notice.

The beauty that I found in New York's underground reminded me of the first time I saw an older Rembrandt painting. I stood in front of the portrait *Man with a Falcon on His Wrist* in the Gothenburg Museum of Art. Taking time to observe the coarse brushstrokes, I stared at the dark-brown painting, perceiving how the face, the strange background, the bird, and the hat altered beneath my gaze. Details emerged that I hadn't noticed at first glance. It was almost like gazing into a bonfire and watching how the flames recreate themselves from one moment to the next.

I rarely seek out those things that I am certain are beautiful because I already know exactly what to expect. It doesn't require any effort, and you aren't surprised. Rembrandt is another matter. His paintings require a response from the viewer. There's so much art that is too obvious. A lovely landscape is sometimes only that. It doesn't display tension, and nothing happens to me when I look at it. In the sewers below the Bronx, I had the opposite experience.

The Raccoon in the Sewer

When it is dark as night the whole day long, it's almost as if time stands still. We padded off and soon came to Broadway. It got warmer. The sewage flowed in from the north, from a pipe joined to our own, and we could hear the cars passing overhead, atop the manhole covers. Each time a wheel hit one, we heard a clang followed by a ringing that resonated in the air before dying out again. Over and over again.

Apparently, people in the Bronx go to the bathroom a lot in the night, and the amount of sewage that we had to wade through increased. But it wasn't annoying. The stench was sharp, but the filth blended with dirty water, garbage, and run-off. I actually consider the smell of dirty diapers to be much worse. As I walked, I looked down into the sewage. The filthy water flowed more quickly than our walking pace so that it came from behind, wrapped itself in eddies around my legs, and continued sailing downward, out toward the treatment plant and the ocean, in the same direction that we were headed. Toilet paper, excrement that had been churned into small pieces, an empty bottle, indistinguishable bits and pieces, and here and there a condom. The toilet paper was almost completely intact. I had witnessed the same thing up in the Himalayas: nature breaks down countless elements, but toilet paper survives the winter intact and manages to stay that way for years.

But nature wasn't completely absent. Suddenly, Alan spotted a raccoon. The fact that he was sopping wet had apparently not dampened his humor, and he called us over. Here in the city, wildlife is usually something seen on television, with the exception of poodles, squirrels, cats, and especially rats, which are everywhere. The raccoon was large and healthy. He seemed somewhat surprised by our visit and scurried off into the tunnel, disappearing.

Steve and I were the only ones to have brought four-gas meters on our excursion. I had bought a new one for the trip, and Steve had taken his old one along. Both meters measured for poisonous carbon-monoxide (CO) and hydrogen-sulfide (H_2S) levels, kept track of available oxygen levels, and had an LEL (Lower Explosive Limit) sensor to measure flammable gases. Steve's meter was partly broken, however, and couldn't measure the oxygen levels.

According to Steve, though, this wasn't a problem. He let Alan carry the four-gas meter. If the meter indicated an absence of explosive gas in the tunnel, he planned to test out oxygen levels by lighting up a cigarette. If the cigarette extinguished by itself, it would mean a lack of oxygen.

After about two or three hours, the alarm around Alan's neck began to sound: a clear, shrill beeping noise. We all jumped. The alarm beeped in short intervals. Alan looked at the gauge and checked the various measurements.

Steve asked Alan to check the batteries. They proved to be almost empty, which accounted for the alarm. Should we continue? We discussed it back and forth. I dimmed my flashlight so as not

---

I stretched out my hand in front of me and couldn't see it. Not even my upper arm. It was almost like I'd ceased to exist.

---

to blind the others, and beamed the light to and fro across the grime-covered faces of Steve, Alan, and Andrew, who emerged partially with each flash. Should we climb out of the tunnel here? But everyone wanted to keep going. Not only were we deterred by the prospect of giving up, we also thought it could be dangerous and careless to climb out in the middle of a congested street. We decided to stay close together and to make do with a single meter.

Wandering through a tunnel is like walking in a monotone landscape, like being at sea far out from land, or in the midst of a thick fog. It's always difficult to know just how far you have come. Without variation in your surroundings for orientation, it's hard to have a sense of cardinal directions or time. Marlow, the narrator in Joseph Conrad's *Heart of Darkness*, who had originally dreamed of reaching the North Pole, reflected on something similar as he sailed along the coast of West Africa at the beginning of his journey: 'Every day the coast looked the same, as though we had not moved; but we passed various places [...].'

As we walked down toward Harlem, increasing amounts of sewage spilled from small pipes or larger tunnels protruding from the walls. Some of the pipes looked clogged. Crusted excrement in various shades of brown hung in bulging formations from the openings. Other pipes contained a steady flow. The influx of sewage had become so extensive that the tunnels and pipeline systems had been expanded to include multiple parallel sections of tunnel. It was a sewage superhighway. The beautiful brick stones that had dominated farther north had now been replaced by concrete.

We switched between tunnels for the fun of it. At one point I found myself walking alone in a tunnel. I decided to turn off my light. It was an endless, permeating darkness down there, much darker than anywhere I have ever been. I stretched out my hand in front of me and couldn't see it. Not even my upper arm. It was almost like I'd ceased to exist. For a few moments, I was encapsulated by complete silence. 'You looked on amazed, and began to suspect yourself of being deaf—then the night came suddenly, and struck you blind as well.' This is not my own description. It is Marlow's, depicting what it's like to be in the jungle. But I understood it. Emerging from the tunnel, I could see the conical lights from the others' head lamps ahead of me in the darkness. I followed the three deep shadows that constituted Steve, Alan, and Andrew. After a while, we were careful to stay in the easternmost pipe. We knew that the pipes would diverge up ahead and one of them would take us down along Exterior Street, heading east. We didn't want to risk missing the tunnel crossing and branching off in the wrong direction.

Blank Spots on the Map

Navigating underground is no easy task. There are few maps of the area, compasses aren't much help, and no one really knows how many tunnels exist below New York. Much less how long they are, or where they all lead. Although the system was built by humans, there doesn't seem to be anyone with an overview. This is one of the things that Will likes. He informed me that he's set aside several years for researching and understanding urban exploration. The underground, he argued, is 'the last frontier in an over-mapped, Google-Earthed world.' Or: it's one of the last bits of Earth that hasn't been discovered or regulated. That means that there are still blank spots on the map. I like that thought. Throughout history, leading voices in each generation have asserted that there's hardly anything left to discover, and yet some new terra incognita always pops up. When Roald Amundsen and his men reached the South Pole—the first people ever to reach *the last place on earth*—*The New York Times* summed up the event as follows: 'The whole world has now been discovered.' They couldn't have been more mistaken. There will always be mysteries tucked beyond the horizon, or below the surface of the ocean, or even beneath the office building of the city's largest newspaper.

Sometime later, a little side tunnel curved off to the left and sloped gradually downward, from Broadway. According to our calculations, this must be Exterior. We were relieved. Not because we had been afraid, but because there was always the chance that something might go wrong. We would arrive at our end point after only three hundred more feet through the tunnel. I was glad that we had managed to avoid danger, but I also felt a bit melancholy. When we spotted the red thread dangling in front of us, I knew that the first stage of our journey had come to an end, but I still looked forward to what was to come. We shouted up, and Will answered from above. He had been waiting for us for four hours, together with Jacki and Brent. There weren't any cars in sight. We climbed easily up the rusty ladder and out into the winter night. I greeted Will and noticed the mist that had accumulated on his glasses.

It felt good coming up out of the sewage pipe, but I immediately missed the sense of excitement and uncertainty from below.

Voltaire Was Right

Just down the street, on Broadway, and opposite the Astral Fitness & Wellbeing Training Center and a run-down gas station encompassed in a fortress of barbed-wire fencing, we came across a twenty-four-hour Dunkin' Donuts. We went in to celebrate with a cup of hot chocolate. The employees were cheerful and bopped around in matching hats and collared T-shirts worn over long-sleeved sweatshirts. There weren't any other customers, so we kind of just took over. Lining the wall were four oversized freezers filled with enormous, brightly colored cakes. We put down our backpacks and for the first time I took a clear look at the faces of my companions. Holy smokes, were we nasty! Steve, Alan, Andrew, and I peeled off our soiled clothes and gathered around some pink tables. The stench from our clothes competed with the sweet smell of the cakes. Steve and I tossed our damaged waders into the trash bin. I half-expected some manager or other to approach us, demanding that we contain our belongings or leave immediately. But New York isn't like other cities. At least not this Dunkin' Donuts, anyway. We sat there, disgusting and stinking to high heaven while a smiling employee mopped away the shit around our feet. Maybe I'm naive, but I think New Yorkers are simply more open to what it means to be different than many other people are.

The hot chocolate tasted heavenly, and as I leaned back, I thought about how rarely I manage to enjoy life exactly where I am, at the moment that I am there. But on this morning it was different. If I could have chosen to be anywhere in the world, I wouldn't have chosen anywhere other than precisely this café, sitting there on a flimsy metal chair at some pink tables. 'Paradise is where I am,' wrote a philosopher—I think it was the French philosopher Voltaire—but unfortunately this is not so easy to achieve. I am a bit more akin to Woody Allen, who said something like, 'When I'm in Paris, I dream about being in New York. And when I'm in New York, I dream of being in Paris.' I often experience this same longing, but not just then. On this morning, Voltaire was right. Sitting there at Dunkin' Donuts felt just like being in paradise.

Steve helps Andrew to empty his hip waders of sewage. Alan (middle) gets a good chuckle.

Steve, face covered in muck, enjoys a cup of hot chocolate at Dunkin' Donuts.

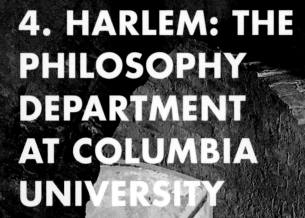

4. HARLEM: THE PHILOSOPHY DEPARTMENT AT COLUMBIA UNIVERSITY

It was Tuesday morning, the second day of our journey. Walking from the Bronx in toward Manhattan makes Manhattan seem isolated. This was the feeling I had, in any case, as Jacki, Alan, Brent, Steve, and I headed south and saw the distant buildings. An island overrun with buildings, where value is created on a large scale and which depends entirely on an influx of people who arrive every morning to work and depart again when the working day is over. The author E. B. White described New York in the 1940s as 'The New York of the commuter—the city that is devoured by locusts each day and spat out each night.' The locusts are the endless stream of people who invade Manhattan each morning. It's no different today.

Many people move to New York while at the peak of their determination, creativity, and career drive, and only leave when these traits have diminished, or when they have children. It's all about fashion, finance, tourism, real estate, shopping, and art. Throughout the last 200 years, Manhattan has been a mystical kind of testing laboratory for architecture, art, and alternative lifestyles, and I have always been fascinated by it.

Amsterdam became the world's most important port of trade thanks to wares such as flowers and porcelain. In Venice, the commerce of spices and costly textiles built the city into a superpower. The main sources of power in New York come from financial services, advertising, and fashion. I am fascinated by the contrast between the dedication to work in these cities throughout history and the trivial commodities that are produced. Some of the world's brightest minds, brandishing the most costly educations, continue year after year to log an astonishing number of hours working on creating media campaigns or loan packages and other such items that society could often do better without. Even so, each of these cities in its prime has been one of the most exciting places to be.

The five of us strolled south for the last mile through the Bronx and toward Harlem River Ship Canal, which separates the Bronx from Harlem and Manhattan.. The shops and restaurants had been decorated for Christmas. I liked walking along the streets, looking at Christmas decorations. They were so much more opulent than back in Norway. There were more Santa Clauses, and they were larger, and made of plastic. They seemed cheerful with their cheeks red as tomatoes. They had been placed in every conceivable nook and cranny, sitting or standing. The most sophisticated of them even nodded their heads.

As far as we could tell, the area was devoid of any grocery stores. But there were a lot of other locations offering their services or wares: Sleepy's, McDonald's, Funerals, Drug Mart, 24 Hr Financial Center, Subway, 99 Cents or More, Beauty Salon, Franco Bakery, Discount Furniture and Rite Aid. Mattresses, funeral services, finance, pharmacies, goods costing around a dollar, and fast food. Neighborhoods like this are often referred to as 'food deserts,' in the sense that it's almost impossible to buy anything other than a pre-cooked meal, such as produce or raw foods. In addition, we noticed an outlet selling tickets for an express bus to Atlantic City, the East Coast's largest gambling haunt. A place to dream oneself away with affordable opportunities to lose money.

We stopped at the end of the Bronx to look out across the canal toward Harlem. A few timeworn barges maneuvered slowly through the water, but otherwise there wasn't much life to be seen so early in the day.

When I was young, I read a story about women living in the Bronx and Harlem who worked in the exclusive shopping centers further south. They would arrive at work early so they could sneak into the book department. There, they would sit and read books they couldn't afford to buy, enjoying themselves until their shifts began. I liked that story, and imagined these women, sunk into deep sofas, each with her own book before opening hours. Maybe it was a true story. If it was, those women must have been happy in those brief moments, sitting and reading.

Jacki and I chatted about the events of the previous night as we crossed Broadway Bridge, the bridge tying the Bronx to Harlem. I liked her. She had pretty brown eyes with a glimmer of curiosity in them. She was drawn to the underground, she said, and had been fascinated by it for a long time. She spoke of the insights she'd gained. 'Crawling through confining, tiny spaces, I realized that the primal nature of human achievement begins with caves,' she said. 'I mean, we have all crawled out of them, historically, as members of the human species. But to be underneath a great city, to know that somewhere above you the generations of modern people rave on, oblivious, while you are at the root, or the source of the story, touching its bones, well—it *is* mythology, isn't it? The universe is transformed. Hands on the rock, peering in the dark, discovering how systems like rivers, drains, tombs, aqueducts come together—yes, I do love being in the labyrinth.'

Above us, atop the bridge, was a small shed where it's possible to sleep. Steve and I had discussed sleeping there after our earlier night session. We looked around. A fence had been constructed to keep people out, but it looked easy enough to climb over. I turned toward Steve, who was walking just behind me, and we briefly debated whether or not to take a snooze up there, but finally decided against it. It was getting too light out, and there were too many people around to risk climbing up and getting inside. Anyone might be tempted to call the police, which would give us something else to think about. On a journey such as ours, it was best to move at night. Steve suggested that we instead take the subway to just past Harlem, to Columbia University, where there were a number of tunnels below campus where we could sleep. We agreed, and Jacki, Alan, Brent, Steve, and I ascended the stairs to the station at 215th Street. On the station platform, we saw a worn-down piece of art from 1991 with the title *Elevated Nature II* shaped on the cement. Elevated nature—could the title have been meant ironically? I went closer to the work and studied it. From close up, I saw that the motif was actually nature. The artist had used sticks to press indentations in the concrete as it had hardened. They almost looked like fossils. From where we stood waiting, we had a view of three factory chimneys that were no longer smoking, worn-down houses covered in graffiti, and parking lots surrounded by barbed wire. I looked out. The industrial remains of this neighborhood were somehow mystical and beautiful. First, the industry took its toll on the environment. Then production was relocated. Now the pipes and buildings have outlived their usefulness. Soon, someone will come with new plans, and the area will be reinvented, but for the time being, nature almost imperceptibly re-establishes itself. It stretches its roots into concrete, improving the living conditions of small animals and plants so they can begin to grow again.

A Subway Car Is Not Just a Subway Car

Aboard the subway, I sat and looked at a poster pasted on the ceiling. It was an advertisement for www.philosophyworks.com, with the tagline: *This poster can make you happier than any other on the subway*, and guaranteed more happiness if you took part in an intensive course. Aristotle would have turned in his grave. For him, the value of experience over a long period of time was the important thing. Next to this was an informational poster for MTA, the company that runs the subway: *Improvements don't just happen.* I had more faith in this message. Not just with regard to the subway, but also to my own life. I am often the most satisfied when I have chosen the more difficult of two alternatives. It's more exciting to walk through New York under and above the ground than to drive the entire route. One question posed to those who have walked to the South Pole is why they didn't just fly there with a helicopter instead? But the entire point is to do it in the most challenging way. A shortcut would render it meaningless.

A subway car is not just a subway car. It's also a micro-society and an expression of the governing authority's desire for punctuality and added value. Passengers should be transported as rapidly as possible to their place of employment, arriving there in order to produce as much as possible. And they should endure sitting tightly compacted and surrendering a bit of their individual freedom. I tried to guess what type of employment the passengers on board had. Some of them were dressed for manual labor and others for the office. I suppose that the wealthiest are transported above ground. It occurred to me that no one spoke with anyone else, and it seemed almost as if everyone were travelling alone. The atmosphere in the car was a strange blend of isolation and imposed fellowship. The subway makes life more efficient, but in return, passengers must conduct themselves accordingly. Some read, some listened to music, but most sat looking down at an angle. I tried to guess what they were looking at, but it seemed that each one had found his or her little dot on the floor that he or she brooded over until he or she arrived.

Two Hearts

I like walking in places that I don't know very well. It's like leaving a part of myself at home. I'm given new coordinates and see places and people for the first time. The impressions are distinct. Walking doesn't cost anything, it isn't even a sport, and all I have to do to start out on an exploration is to put one leg in front of the other. Once, when walking along Lake Geneva, I met one of the world's leading heart surgeons, Magdi Habib Yacoub. Magdi is an Egyptian immigrant to England, and his story is the opposite of obscurity and despair. At the time that I met him, he had performed around 20,000 heart operations and 2,600 heart-and-lung transplants. Instead of operating solely on those who could pay for his services, he had put aside a few months of each year to undertake operations in impoverished parts of Africa. Ten years prior, he had transplanted a new heart into a two-year-old girl. When he disconnected her own heart during the operation, he left it intact in her body. After about ten years, the borrowed heart stopped functioning the way it should, and the situation was once again a matter of life and death. Magdi was summoned. He disconnected heart number two and reconnected her own heart again, which had in the meantime grown and become strong within her body. The girl was revived shortly thereafter.

I asked him what motivated him to continue his work now that he was retired, and he answered with a smile: 'I have become addicted to seeing people recover.' As we parted, he gave me some advice: 'Go walking every day.' I have followed his advice.

The subway stopped at 116th Street. The station was nice and clean. Gorgeous white and blue ceramic tiles adorned the station walls. We hopped off and walked to Tom's Restaurant, just south of Columbia, a traditional diner offering only that thin American variety of coffee, but which also had delicious fried eggs and pancakes. In a city whose inhabitants stock their pantries with health food, and where the city's big health commissioner, Thomas Farley, has stated, 'I think what people fear is getting fat,' it was liberating to actually find a decent meal that could stick to your ribs. We hadn't eaten properly since the previous day. I looked at the others. We were pretty wasted and tired after the long, sleepless night in the sewers, but the waiter didn't take it personally. We ordered pancakes and scrambled eggs.

After breakfast, we walked to the university at 125th Street and in through the main gate that faces Broadway, intent on getting some sleep. We were met by an elegant entryway and impressive buildings inside. I glanced over at *The Thinker* by Rodin, where he sat immersed in his own world, every visible muscle in his body tensed, his head resting on his right hand. The sculpture was originally made to illustrate Dante before the gates of hell, but here it illustrates the power of thought. Dante sits there as a daily reminder of what is expected of the students. Like Harvard, Yale, and Princeton, Columbia attempts to overcome its relatively brief heritage by mimicking the same classical and Roman ideals that characterize British universities, and thereby achieve a respectable façade. I would say it succeeded here.

Steve informed us that some parts of the American nuclear-weapons program, the Manhattan Project, were started in basements beneath Columbia in the 1930s. Up to seven hundred researchers worked in secret to split atoms, and at one point the university's football team was involved in lugging several tons of uranium. The work culminated three years later when the nuclear bomb was dropped on Japan.

Before the university was built, a psychiatric hospital had occupied the grounds. That building has been moved, but only a few feet away. Steve likes the idea that the university is the continuation of the psychiatric hospital. 'I just think it's super-cool that Columbia is planted in the footprint of an old asylum.'

We ambled across the courtyard and entered the Department of East Asian Studies, a building located just next to Hamilton Hall. We walked through the door to the Center for East Asian Studies and continued down the stairs, where we passed some workers. I think they were filling up a hot-chocolate or soda machine, but whenever we were somewhere where we shouldn't be,

---

When you're on an expedition, your behavior more and more begins to resemble that of an animal. I crept over to another corner, sat on my knees and I, too, relieved myself.

I never looked too closely at anyone. We had reached the cellar, but one of the doors that was supposed to lead us further was closed. Steve picked the lock. He had done it before. We entered what might have been the central heating facility of the university. From there, we climbed up a small ladder and crept along between pipes and large tanks. A constant clanking noise sounded in the pipes. On one side of me was a wall and on the other, hot pipes from the heating system. I walked slowly. After about fifty feet we arrived at another ladder. Ascending, we entered a dark room with a low ceiling. The air was humid and musty, but there was a lot of floor space. In addition to the constant clunking in the pipes, we could suddenly hear voices. The room echoed and we kept still as mice. Someone spoke in French above us, and we assumed that we must be under the Buell Hall, or French Institute. Steve told us that this building was left over from the old asylum, and the tunnel we had taken to get there was a remnant of the asylum as well. Unpacking our sleeping bags and mats, the five of us made space for ourselves away from each other and hunkered down to sleep. Just before nodding off, I heard someone peeing in the corner of the room. The darkness made it impossible to know who it was. It seemed unnatural to piss in such a magnificent building, but on the other hand, it was better than peeing into your pants, and anyway, hardly anyone ever came down here. When you're on an expedition, your behavior more and more begins to resemble that of an animal. I crept over to another corner, sat on my knees and I, too, relieved myself.

The Importance of Opening Doors

We slept like logs and only woke up later that afternoon. Steve wanted to sleep longer; he had his own rhythm and was a bit stressed out about it, but we insisted we had to move on. When his telephone rang, he rasped into the microphone: 'I can't talk right now! I'm in the underground.'

We knew the way back, and though we had come to Columbia to sleep and not to research, we agreed that we would try to discover another way out of the central heating facility than the one we'd entered. After all, we didn't come on this trip to go the same way twice! Steve knew about an alternative exit that led more directly out of the building. We passed through a small hallway, but the hatch that we wanted to climb through had been secured with new locks on the outside. Apparently there had been too many visitors. We turned and retraced our steps. A battered door near where we had slept offered a refreshing alternative. But this is where we had heard voices when we were lying down to sleep a few hours earlier. We weren't especially eager to get busted at this point. The ceiling was low and I stooped and walked over to the door, curled my right hand together like a stethoscope, laid my ear up against it, and listened. It was quiet. I waited for half a minute; there was still no noise, only the clanking in the pipes. I pushed open the door. We ambled through halls and corridors. Steve named the various buildings that we were walking beneath, but I only heard some of what he said. Philosophy Hall, Buell Hall, the Institute for French Studies. What would happen if we were spotted? Would they just escort us out or would we be reported to the police for breaking and entering? I didn't know, and I decided not to speculate. We criss-crossed here and there, opened various doors to find a way out, went in the wrong direction, retraced our steps, went back again and tried a new direction.

'One of these takes you out through the philosophy building, but apparently this is a dead end. Like philosophy,' commented Steve. In the end, we arrived at a large, wide door that was unlocked. We slipped through. I glanced around, wondering where we were. Up ahead a sign informed us we were in the building that housed the Philosophy Department. I joked with my companions about the importance of opening doors that other people don't bother opening. Maybe we were in the process of finding answers to some of life's big questions?

Still at the level of the cellar, we came to a staircase leading upward. We hadn't met any other people since passing the two maintenance workers earlier. Finally at the top, we pushed open another door and were surprised by a large crowd of people. Philosophy was having a party. We stood looking in at the fifty or so guests. No one noticed us. They were dressed almost all alike. Not too nice, but just unkempt and informal enough. Here they were scraggly in a more orchestrated way than people in the Bronx. They were also thinner. And they all seemed more self-satisfied. I thought about the bulky, black shoes of imitation leather with thick rubber soles that had been the standard in the Bronx. There weren't many of those here. The girls here had put up their hair a bit haphazardly and some of the guys had day-old stubble. It was exactly how I pictured students and professors of a philosophy department to dress for a party. The mood was good and unrestrained. I walked into the room and made a small round, and some people glanced at me a bit strangely, but most of them didn't seem bothered. There was an abundance of food and cheap wine.

I glanced over at a professorial-looking chap in a tweed jacket standing nearby. Several students were gathered around him. Maybe he had answers to the questions I'd been asking myself for a long time? Was Sigmund Freud wrong—the father of psychoanalysis, who had dreamed of achieving as significant a place in the field of human psychology as the Renaissance mathematician and astronomer Copernicus and the English naturalist Charles Darwin had achieved in their fields—when he assumed that happiness and unhappiness were opposites? What has happened with happiness from the time that Aristotle described how to be happy up until the time Prozac was invented?

Could we be the first society in which we are unhappy because we are happy?

I already had an idea about the answer to this last question, and I think it has to be: a lot. When Aristotle described happiness, *eudaimonia*, which actually means to be possessed by a good spirit, he wasn't thinking about a short-lived feeling of happiness: 'For one swallow does not make a summer, nor does one fine day; similarly one day or brief time of happiness does not make a person entirely happy.' Both in New York and back home, the prevailing attitude is often about experiencing a steady flow of happy moments. It is rarely about remaining happy. The hunt for moments of happiness has become something resembling an ideology—a rather general mindset and vision about what is important in life, and also about what is the right way to live. Could we be the first society in which we are unhappy because we are happy? In Aristotle's day, a life lived morally ranked higher than a happy life, but it seems like the reverse is now true. Immediate and transitory happiness is often at the top of the list. I think we are walking on thin ice and could use the help of the people at the philosophy party to understand what the history of philosophy has to teach us about balance, composure, and living a life of meaning.

The American Dream

Sipping a cold glass of beer in the springtime sun, kicking back a pill, or going shopping or ice-skating at Rockefeller Center are all enjoyable, but these aren't happiness in the Aristotelian sense. According to Aristotle, happiness comes from succeeding in life. Like Buddha, he maintained that happiness is an action that requires that you live in accordance with your values, and that you have the material goods that you need, not only 'for one random moment, but throughout your entire life.' To achieve this, you must utilize all of your capabilities. Not just a portion of them, not like the top athlete or banker or data nerd who are just doing their thing.

The American dream is founded on the idea that all people have the opportunity to succeed and to be happy. This dream is older than the USA. Philosophers such as Confucius, Socrates, and Plato also believed that anyone could achieve happiness. But Aristotle included some important requirements. He highlighted a litany of necessary external conditions to happiness: wealth, children, beauty, and friends, all of which exclude large swaths of people.

The debate about happiness and how we should live a happy life is no longer the sole domain of philosophy, nowadays. It has instead become a job for psychologists, pharmacists, politicians, and media columnists. This is a pity. The focus has slowly shifted away from *we* and *should*, which was the starting point for philosophy, to *I* and *must*, which are the premises for today's experts. This shift took about 2,500 years. For the most part, today's philosophers are more specialized and tend to focus on increasingly more abstract questions, so that Steve was right: philosophy can be a dead end.

Columbia was involved in building the nuclear bomb, making it possible to wipe out entire cities at the push of a button. Drawing closer to questions of meaning in life is more complicated.

I stood immersed in my own thoughts when Steve came over and urged me to fill up on drinking water, which gave me something else to think about. The bar was tantalizing, but we had so far managed to avoid getting into trouble. If we took it too far, someone might start asking what exactly we were up to. With our backpacks, dirty clothes, and a splatter of dust at our feet, Jacki, Brent, Alan, Steve, and I clearly stood out from the other guests. We were a merry bunch. I doubted that anyone would trouble us if we stayed, but it was too early for a party, anyway, and we decided to continue on our way.

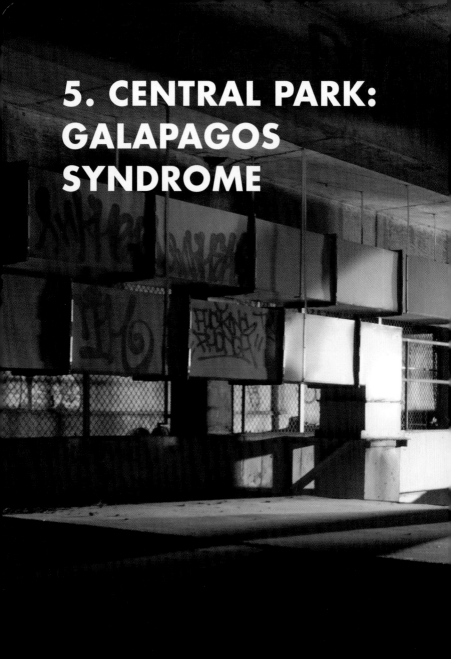

5. CENTRAL PARK: GALAPAGOS SYNDROME

We decided to pop down to 107th Street where Alan knew of a place with good Mexican food, *Taqueria y Fonda La Mexicana*. Dusk had fallen outside. Christmas lights twinkled along Amsterdam Avenue. The Christmas decorations were garish here as well, but there was no doubt that we were now in an area with more expensive wares. The first things I noticed upon entering the restaurant was a Christmas-decorated disco ball hanging from the ceiling, a marbleized white bar made of plastic, and a Coca-Cola refrigerator filled with beer. Two guys were frying meat and sweating buckets in the open kitchen just next to the entrance. Beside them hung a picture of independence fighter Emiliano Zapata with the inscription *Tierra y Libertad!*—he was the man of the people against those in power. I can't quite put my finger on the reasons why, but I was immediately certain we were in a place that was going to serve us good food. And we were so ravenous that it would have tasted good in any case.

Steve and I talked and planned. We were both eager for a bit of variation from our previous routes. The goal of the journey was not to traverse the city as efficiently as possible, but to experience more than sewage and heating systems. In other words, to experience the subway, train, and water tunnels as well. Steve's suggestion for later that evening was for us to drop down to the Lower East Side subway station at Delancey Street and attempt to enter the subway tunnels from there. I liked the idea. Night is the best time to venture into subway tunnels, when there are few people at the stations and when the express trains, which run along the two middle tracks, have stopped for the day. It's also good early in the evenings at stations where there aren't too many travelers on the platforms.

We still had some time to kill before it would be late enough to enter the subway tunnels. Steve and I decided to ride the subway down to the south end of Central Park and take a turn under the park. Jacki, Brent, and Alan came along. I liked the feeling of not having a fixed route to follow as long as we were generally moving toward the sea. Journeys are more exciting when they have a geographic goal. Inside of the subway car, milk-chocolate-colored models with nice teeth smiled at us from the walls and guaranteed the subway passengers a happy stay on Aruba. The small Caribbean island had bought up almost all of the advertisement space in the car. But the question is whether tourists will find happiness there, I thought. Maybe the feeling of happiness rather comes from dreaming about Aruba before you get there? And after you've returned home and have forgotten about the intestinal bug? Of course, hopefully something nice happens on Aruba, but for my own part, experiences that I consider happy were rarely only made up of good things that happened. Rather, after I've achieved a bit of distance from those experiences, it's easier for me to forget or to laugh about the negative aspects and enjoy the pleasant ones. I'm free to embellish my memories, and that's all right.

Many years ago, together with a girl I was dating at the time, I climbed up Store Skagastølstind, the third-highest mountain in Norway. We had nice weather as we began our ascent, but further up we were met with sleet, and by the time we turned at the summit, it had gotten dark. We were surrounded by steep precipices on all sides. I tripped on a rappelling attachment and after that we agreed to stay up there overnight, clothed only in our meager climbing gear. It was a long, wet, and very cold night. We did everything we could to stay warm. We flailed our arms, hopped up and down, and shadow-boxed throughout the night, but we were freezing anyway. It was not an enjoyable night up there—on the contrary—but when the sun rose and we managed to descend safely together, the experience had brought us closer together.

Memories of past days and nights blend into each other and can easily start looking the same. But spending a night together under dramatic circumstances makes one night stand out from all the others.

Achieving Happiness by Being Better Off than Your Neighbor

Joys that are meant to end are often far more rewarding than joys that are supposed to last indefinitely. Travelling to Aruba, sharing a good meal with a friend, watching a great film, or passing through New York are hopefully memories that I can recall with pleasure. But most of what I purchase for long-term use quickly loses its appeal as my interest in the new acquisition wanes. The advertisements I notice as I pass through the city cater mostly to transient pleasures and suggest that marketers believe that we all share the same dreams: better cars, thinner bodies, more exclusive vacations, more money, larger homes, and renown.

If I had to choose a common denominator for the advertisements' messages, I would say they are about happiness. About doing better than one's neighbor or than someone else who you could compare yourself to. And about being happy for these reasons. Perhaps this isn't so strange after all? A survey of students at Harvard revealed that participants would rather be the richest paupers in a poor neighborhood than the poorest millionaires in a rich one. Obesity is another topic that has been researched extensively. 'In simple terms, it feels okay to be fat when our loved ones—or other people with whom we normally identify—are fat as well,' concludes Nattavudh Powdthavee, a research economist and author of *The Happiness Equation*. Well-educated people are more likely to feel overweight than less-educated people. The background to this is that people with a higher education have a thinner standard than others. This might be part of the reason that people in this part of the city are thinner than those farther north. Nonetheless, I believe that the people behind the advertisements are wrong. Most people are looking for something better and deeper in their lives—such as good friendships, love, good health, and knowledge acquired from their experiences over time—rather than immediate pleasure. Life would hold little meaning if the priorities of advertising were as important as they claim to be.

Slowly Count to Ten

In 1990, when Børge Ousland and I reached the North Pole, an American spy plane happened to fly over us the day after we arrived. The pilots were probably just as surprised as we were to see someone else at the North Pole. As a gesture of kindness toward two famished polar explorers, they dropped a box of food before continuing on. After fifty-eight days in temperatures of around -70° Fahrenheit, most of the fat had burned off of our bodies, as well as muscle mass. We had stretched our days from twenty-four to thirty hours to reach the pole, so that we could walk for seventeen-hour stages at a time. The cold and hunger had made it almost impossible to sleep at times. We opened the box, divided the food from the airplane between us, and laid it out on our sleeping mats. I was about to start devouring the food, but Børge suggested we shouldn't begin eating at once but wait for a moment. Slowly count to ten internally and then eat. Show collective restraint. Remind each other that satisfaction is also about sacrifice. It felt strange to wait. I have seldom felt so rich as I did in that moment.

If You Aim for Happiness, You Miss the Mark

Inside the subway car, next to the ad for Aruba, another dream was being sold: *I teach 'getting ahead.' How to reach your own potential.* Dr. Tilokie Depoo, an academic management professional and Dean of Business Programs at the Metropolitan College of New York. Dr. Depoo promises a lot. Aristotle was right when he claimed that happiness comes as a result of what you do, and not from actions that have happiness as their goal.

I find that I am often disappointed when I do something first and foremost for the purpose of being happy. At times, it can even seem like the pursuit of happiness is the most common cause of people's unhappiness. Because the shortest way to a goal is rarely straight ahead. If I had thought about the top of Everest when I

A business that is only concerned with profit usually turns bad; a country with politicians who want to plan everything down to the detail ends up in chaos; and those artists that I know who want, more than anything, to create a timeless piece of work are quickly outdated.

---

first started out, I would never have reached it and been able to come down again. Those who always try to be original are rarely that. Those who think they'll find happiness by reading a self-help book end up constantly buying more and more self-help books, and those who just want to be good people often don't end up as good people. A business that is only concerned with profit usually turns bad; a country with politicians who want to plan everything down to the detail ends up in chaos; and those artists that I know who want, more than anything, to create a timeless piece of work are quickly outdated.

As a publisher, I've often noticed that the more an author thinks about sales and marketing before he has even begun writing, the worse the book is, and the less it sells.

We had only been underway for just over a day, but it felt like much longer. The sense of time changes when there's always something new happening, as it did on this trip. Arriving at 59th Street and Columbus Circle, we hopped off the subway. Elaborate mosaics adorned the station, and the first one I noticed was a small relief of the boat of Christopher Columbus, the *Santa Maria*. A green sea, blue sky, three masts, four sails, and three birds circling the ship. On the way out of the station, we were met by a real-estate advertisement: *Where You Live Matters*. When we reached the street, we stood and looked out at the many buildings in the city bearing the name Trump. I told Steve about Donald Trump's last wife. When asked whether she would have married The Donald if he hadn't been so rich, she had given the best answer: 'Do you think he would have married me if I hadn't been so beautiful?'

'That's how it is,' answered Steve.

We walked down 59th Street along the park. I perused the discreet signs at every park entrance. Dr. Lawrence D. Jagger: Advanced Dermatology Associates, Medical Hair Restoration, Exhale Mind and Body Spa, and Implant Esthetic, Reconstructive Dentistry. Inherent in the names was a pledge that one could be remade. I'm guessing there aren't so many doctors and therapists around here who simply tell a patient that he's healthy and can go home and need not ever come back again.

I've never seen such a high concentration of good helpers in such a small circumference. If I lived in a district surrounded by therapists, I imagine it would be hard to think of myself as healthy. During his visit to a tuberculosis sanatorium in Davos, Hans Castorp, the main character in Thomas Mann's novel *The Magic Mountain*, is queried by a doctor whether he feels healthy. He does, but the doctor is relentless. 'Do you feel healthy,' he asks again. Well, doesn't he, actually? Castorp allows himself to be persuaded he is sick. He is committed to the sanatorium and becomes a patient for seven years. Outside the snow falls, day after day. Life at the sanatorium quickly becomes the normal life for Hans, and he develops the fear that they will one day find him too healthy to remain.

The best place to live, according to Aristotle, is the place where you can realize yourself. He emphasized that only a select few people were tasked with having big thoughts, and a life without slaves would make the task of self-realization difficult. Aristotle's ideas live on in their own way. Slavery has been abolished, but most of the people who can afford it in this neighborhood employ people of other ethnic origins as cleaners, personal assistants, and chauffeurs in a bid to free up time. That's in addition to highly paid therapists and doctors. Some of the wealthiest people have so many helpers that they can't even manage them, and must employ someone to do just that. Those who have found success— and that includes most of the folks around 59th Street—are often not in doubt that the big thoughts are reserved for people like themselves, and few others. On the other hand, people usually tend to believe they are smarter than the average Joe.

A Little Galapagos Syndrome

Walking along the south end of Central Park, one of the most exclusive stretches in the world, I eventually started to feel the same thing that I did when I hiked around the Galapagos twenty-five years ago. There we witnessed first-hand the building blocks for Charles Darwin's studies on evolution. When he visited the cluster of islands in 1835, he saw, just as I did one and a half centuries later, how the birds and turtles, plants and reptiles of an island had not only developed differently than on the mainland far away, but also how the flora and fauna differed from island to island. If Darwin had come to Manhattan in our times, he may certainly have registered something similar: small communities that have developed over time to be independent of the outside world. Central Park and some of the other wealthier areas not only seem isolated from North America, but also from the city itself. With the result, I thought as I plodded along through the crowds in Manhattan, that there is now a little Galapagos Syndrome. Not in a biological sense, but culturally.

The late American sociologist Robert K. Merton wrote about something that he called the Matthew effect, named after one of the four evangelists: the rich get richer, the poor get poorer. Maybe the world is a bit fairer than Merton declared it to be? I think it is. As soon as people become as rich as the inhabitants in this part of town, they begin spending more money, energy, and time to recreate themselves in their own image. Clothing, cars, interiors, health, sex, beauty, and body. Age is postponed, no matter the cost. Many have trouble accepting death, and deny that it will happen to them.

Adam Smith, the Scottish philosopher and pioneer of political economy—who is beloved by right-wing politicians who have not necessarily read his work, and shunned by the left-wingers because he is liked by people on the right—wrote about the same thing. He argued that once the wealthy have filled their bellies with food and fulfilled their primary needs, they would begin to squander their wealth: 'The capacity of his stomach bears no proportion to the immensity of his desire.' Not only will the rich man use up his money on all kinds of things he doesn't need, but also he will wish to do it excessively, in stupid ways, and will make a fool of himself. It's as though the ability to purchase, as soon as one has reached a certain point, is inversely proportional to the ability to enjoy what one has purchased. Like X- and Y-axes that cross one another, X, the ability to purchase, goes up while Y, the joy of what one has, goes down. Smith employs the term 'an invisible hand' to describe the mechanism that ensures that, in this way, fortunes are redistributed and return in the end to the people. It is not the world's task to be just, but at the end of the day, it seems like the world is just after all.

'No pleasure is in itself evil, but the things which produce certain pleasures entail annoyances many times greater than the pleasures themselves,' wrote Epicurus already some 2,300 years ago. I know an 82-year-old art collector residing just south of Central Park who is a living example of Epicurus' teachings. After using Viagra for many years, the man is no longer satisfied with the effects. A few years ago, he wanted to get a penis implant so that, at the push of a button, he would be able to have an erection. The first doctors he asked refused. It was too risky for an old man, they said. His wife recommended he let it be. 'You have had your run,' she said. But he went ahead anyway and, after the operation, his wound became infected. He remained at the hospital for several months and was near death. According to his wife, the implant has never worked. At least not that she knows of.

Life on a Hamster Wheel

We had discussed sleeping under Central Park for a night if it worked out. There's a tunnel located about one hundred twenty feet below the park that was created as part of a larger strategy. But when the plan was initiated, it turned out that they didn't need the tunnel after all. It has never been used. It just sits there. 'It just seems crazy that in this super-developed, ritzy area there is an abandoned, unused tunnel,' said Steve. We passed the New York Athletic Club. A big place, and quite posh. We went in to ask whether we could go into the cellar to look for traces of a river running beneath the park and the club. The security guard knew about the river but, surprisingly, denied us entry. It was a private club, with a necktie policy. Just to be perfectly clear, they had indicated this with two signs on either side of the doors. The guard was dressed in a wonderfully tailored uniform and it struck me how kind he was. I wonder if there are other similar places where the doorman spends so much time explaining to someone who looks like an outlier why he cannot enter one of the city's most exclusive clubs to look for traces of a river.

Virtually everything that happens above ground has its subterranean counterpart. In a way, the ruins and the active underground structures also tell about the history of New York. All of the pipes, tunnels, and secret passageways bear witness to everything that has taken place in the city since someone started building here. This historic underbelly quickly gets forgotten as the new changes keep occurring.

I liked that he dealt respectfully with us. Of course I liked it. Almost everyone wants to be handled with respect. Perhaps he treated us so properly because he understood that we were no ordinary bums? Maybe he thought that you never know who is disguised beneath a shabby façade? We exited the club and made our way into the park to look for air valves to flip open for a glimpse at what was hidden below.

It was a clear, starry night; the moon lighted up large stretches of the park, as did the Christmas lights and the lights from the surrounding buildings. No cost was spared in this part of town.

I was overwhelmed by the beauty of the city. The houses changed with the light around them, but not even the buildings were static. They change, too, albeit over a longer-term than we can observe. The concrete, walls, and metal are affected by changes in humidity and pollution, blasts and vibrations in the neighborhood.

There is a type of architecture beneath everything that I see. It's one that has been constructed and rebuilt several times, quickly and pragmatically, for the sake of all that goes on above ground, without thought to the underground aesthetic. Virtually everything that happens above ground has its subterranean counterpart. In a way, the ruins and the active underground structures also tell about the history of New York. All of the pipes, tunnels, and secret passageways bear witness to everything that has taken place in the city since someone started building here. This historic underbelly quickly gets forgotten as the new changes keep occurring. Is it possible that our attitudes and relationships to the past will change? Many years from now, the buildings that I now look at will be viewed as antiquated and outdated. It will be profitable to tear down and reconstruct. More changes will take place below the ground, but some parts of what used to be will remain. Perhaps, one day, some people will be interested in what is down there below ground, and they will begin to dig in order to unearth and understand the course of history in the city. A history that was about growth, politics, and optimism, followed by a history of pessimism, ambition, corruption, exploitation, personal ups and downs, technology, and feats of engineering. Stories about the civilization of a society always have a parallel version that is about barbarism.

I looked around and wondered about how much it must have cost to create the fortunes that financed the surrounding apartments. There must have been a lot of people who believed they would finally find happiness with an apartment overlooking Central Park. And probably they were happy for a while. Happiness can be bought, to a point. But from a broader perspective, those people who live at the most expensive addresses in New York are just like the rest of us: a bunch of folks, each on his own hamster wheel. If we're able to get up to twelve miles an hour, we then try to achieve thirteen. If we are in worse shape, we lower the speed. The hamster wheel can be regulated both upward and downward, but it's not so easy hopping off as long as the wheel is spinning.

As a publisher, I have the impression that there are a lot of journalists who would have liked to be authors, many artists who dream of being DJs, and actors who would have liked to record a jazz album. And there are a countless number of people who have achieved something in their field who dream about starting up a restaurant or bar. They even imagine they've gotten so good at everything they do that they will earn money by doing it. In general, everyone I know who has become wealthy and passed the ten million-dollar mark thinks he or she is an expert on red wine and foreign policy. These people have suddenly become so self-confident and believe that they know better than The President exactly what's needed to breathe life into the American economy, or what the solution is for unemployment in Europe. The transformation, not of knowledge, but of one's self-perception, can change in an instant. I know this not only because I have seen it among others, but also because I have seen it in myself. Maybe there are many people who could borrow the epitaph of a man Adam Smith tells about: *I did well, I could have done better, here I lie.*

Out of Here—That's My Goal

One ambition that generations of humans have passed on to one another, and which is responsible for spurring the world to move ahead, is the desire to be any other place than where we are. Franz Kafka's short story 'The Departure' illustrates our desire to be transported to another place, or even to be another person, and I recognize myself in it. A man saddles his horse and gets ready to ride away, but the servant stops him at the gate and asks, 'Where is the master going?'

'I don't know. Just out of here, just out of here. Out of here, nothing else, it's the only way I can reach my goal.'

'So you know your goal?' he is asked.

'Yes, I've just told you. Out of here—that's my goal.'

Maybe our journey isn't only about being somewhere else, but is also a desire to be *someone* else? I believe so. When I am walking along in mucky clothes, disappearing underground, uncertain of what might occur at any moment, and am carrying everything that I need on my back, I'm not the same Erling Kagge that I am back home. Normal is scoured away. I am not headed to meet anyone that I know, my telephone is turned off, and there is no one waiting for me at home or at the office. I don't even know where I am going to be sleeping the next night.

Jacki, Brent, Alan, Steve, and I discovered some air ventilators along the ground just past the zoo in Central Park, and took down the crowbars from our packs. Alan kept watch while Steve and I took our crowbars in hand to lift up and open vent after vent, but they were all locked from below. We peered down with our lights. Below us were grey, empty rooms of concrete. We tried

---

The cover was placed neatly on top again and we followed the Norwegian cabin rule, which states that you must leave a place in the same condition that you found it. We set a southward course.

---

to lift up the edges, look at what we could, but to no avail. I have learned that, in such cases, you just have to keep trying. There is almost always an untried possibility. The others weren't ready to throw in the towel yet, either.

There were several other hatches a few feet away, and we checked them methodically. Stuck the crowbars down and felt if they would give. In the end, we found one that hadn't been locked. We flipped it open and pushed it carefully aside. Manholes covers are round and can't fall down into the holes, but these were square. If we lost one, it could fall with a bang onto the floor of the room below us, and would leave a large opening that other passers-by might stumble into. All of us wanted to avoid this, and Steve and I were deeply concentrated as we removed it. With Alan standing guard, Steve, Brent, Jacki, and I climbed down. One passage was so narrow that, given my own height of six feet three inches, I couldn't get through. The others rummaged about for a few minutes before surfacing again. The cover was placed neatly on top again and we followed the Norwegian cabin rule, which states that you must leave a place in the same condition that you found it. We set a southward course.

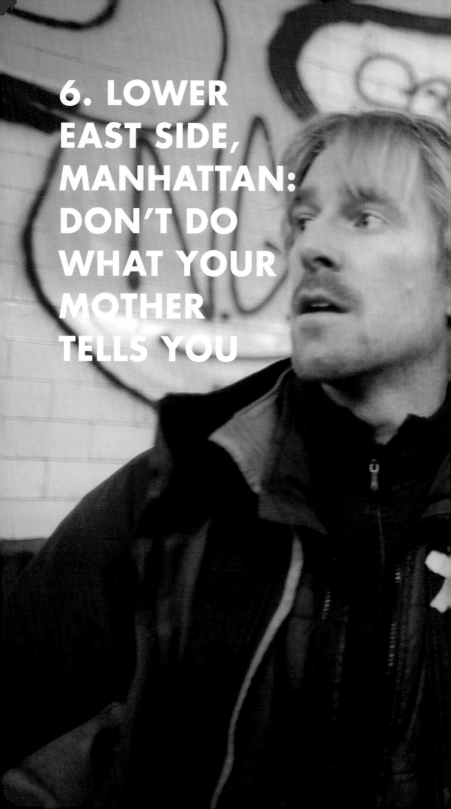

6. LOWER EAST SIDE, MANHATTAN: DON'T DO WHAT YOUR MOTHER TELLS YOU

Before we began our expedition, I asked Moses Gates if he had any advice for us. Moses is a good friend of Steve's and an experienced urban explorer. He is also one of the founders of www.sexonbridges.com, where readers post photos of people, preferably themselves, having sex on the tops of bridges. Steve and I had each crashed on sofas at his place in the days before our expedition to pack our things and make last-minute preparations. Moses replied to me that he only had three pieces of advice: don't get too close to the electric tracks, don't get hit by any trains, and don't multitask while walking along the tracks. It was good advice.

We had been underway for a bit more than a day and we only had one problem: there were too many people who wanted to join us. We had to narrow it down. Jacki, Brent, and Alan were already part of our group, and now *The New York Times* wanted to send along a photographer. Andrew wanted to film, something that was already a part of our plan. Will also showed up. Since he had been so kind as to keep watch at the manhole in Exterior Street, he would be allowed on this stage of the journey. If Moses could have seen us now, he might have given us a fourth piece of advice: don't put too many people into a single tunnel.

Everyone who wanted to come along met up at the McDonald's just opposite Delancey Street Station. Steve asked me whether it was time to have a talk about safety below ground, and the plan going forward. I agreed.

'The most important thing here is not getting killed,' began Steve, and continued, 'so don't get close to the electric tracks. If a train comes, get out of there. In the worst case, you might have to stand between two electric tracks with trains passing on both sides. Then you will be spotted, which isn't good, but it's better than getting killed.' Steve went on to say that we were too many people. Andrew, Steve, and I would go ahead, and the others could follow behind as best as they could.

Alan didn't like what he heard. It seemed too dangerous to him. He didn't want to be a part of a large group that could get separated in the tunnel. His photographer agreed. The speech had the desired effect. Alan was fun to talk with, he never complained, and I thought he would be able to write a good story, so I felt a bit bad about it. 'I have to follow my heart,' he explained. 'And what you are proposing now is crazy. I don't want to come. See you later.' Alan had previously worked in Baghdad to cover the Iraq war for *The New York Times* and therefore knew something about risk management—the dangers of running through a dark subway tunnel with four tracks, each electrically powered with six hundred and twenty-five volts, did not weigh up against putting an interesting story into print. Thus the article idea was benched, since Alan couldn't imagine writing about an expedition that he was no longer a part of.

For Alan, reason took the upper hand. In *The Divine Comedy*, one rightly ends up in a high level of hell for 'placing desire/and passion higher than reason,' and this is probably where Steve and I belonged. This is also the location of Helena, the world's most beautiful woman in her day, as well as the queen Cleopatra and the great centurion Achilles, who was driven to his death by love. Also of Francesca, who cheated on her husband with her lover Paolo, and laments: 'There is no greater sorrow/Than to be mindful of the happy time/In misery.' Dante is gripped by the passion of Francesca and Paolo. He appears to identify with them and grows weak upon considering the longing that has led them both, and himself as well, toward such unhappiness.

Francesca rejects Dante's sentiments. Just like Dante's companion Virgil, she is dead and lost. After her death, Francesca has seen the opportunities that she allowed to slip past in life. Dante, on the other hand, like us, is still alive, living with the uncertainty of all of his neglected chances.

Just Cause You Can't See Don't Mean Ain't Nothing There

The platform at Delancey Station was dotted with commuters on their way home after work on this early Tuesday evening. We boarded a subway to try our luck at Bowery Station instead. In the subway car, someone was reading that autumn's hottest book sensation about the burdens and temptations of too much liberty: Jonathan Franzen's *Freedom*. I had finished reading it just before my trip to New York, and it had reminded me of the Swiss psychiatrist and psychoanalyst Carl Jung's claim that the most powerful forces in a home are the parents' unrealized dreams. One sentence from the book had already been cited internationally in the media: 'The personality susceptible to the dream of limitless freedom is a personality also prone, should the dream ever sour, to misanthropy and rage.' The freedom of the main characters in *Freedom* is mostly a freedom *from* something. A negative freedom. 'Freedom from guilt, anxiety, boredom, anger, purposelessness,' while our journey was more about the freedom *toward* something. A positive freedom toward fulfilling a dream, toward exploring and discovering, and a desire to understand some of the reasons why we act as we do. I have always preferred this kind of freedom to the freedom from things that I don't like.

Bowery Station was only one stop away. We got off the subway, but while the other passengers continued toward the exits, we remained on the platform and prepared to follow the next subway through the tunnels. Somewhere deep in my mind I could hear the command my mother gave me as a small boy: 'Never walk on the railway tracks.'

Slipping into the subway tunnels is a piece of cake. You stand at the end of the platform as the subway departs, and then you hop down onto the track and jog into the tunnel behind the train. As the last wagon in the silver row of passenger cars passed by in its direction north, both Steve and I jumped down simultaneously. Further inside the tunnel it was pitch-black. It was a large open space—four subways could pass through at the same time—but we could barely see more than five or six feet ahead of us. The others followed and came up behind. 'Just cause you can't see don't mean ain't nothing there,' they say about the New York underground at the start of the 2008 comic strip *Pitch Black*, by Youme Landowne and Anthony Horton.

To start off, there was a lot of broken glass. We couldn't see it, but we could hear it splintering underfoot. And garbage and left-over food. Waiting passengers toss away half-eaten burgers and bagels. A real smorgasbord for rats—this is the reason they like to live in the subway tunnels near the stations. Farther away from the station, we mostly walked on gravel. Our eyes became accustomed to the murkiness and I could make out the tracks around us. If anyone turned on a light, we were instructed to point it downward and not up ahead. Steve explained that track workers always placed red or orange lights on a track to warn oncoming trains to slow down or stop for the construction work.

A train came toward us. I heard the sound from far away and, for a split second, I couldn't tell from which direction it came. But as the sound increased, we heard that it was headed in the opposite direction from where we were heading. We crammed together behind a cement wall so as not to be seen when the subway passed. Two or three seconds later, a train swept through at full speed. The air pressure pushed against me. If I'd stretched out my arm, I might even have been able to touch it. The lights from the windows splashed into the tunnel; it was a beautiful sight. I could sense a tingling in my body. It was almost like being a twelve-year-old and pulling pranks again.

Andrew, Steve, and I continued. We passed by a station that had been shut down. Trash littered the platform. Apparently some homeless people camped here every now and then. Earlier in the day we had talked about catching up on our own sleep at an abandoned station. Should we try sleeping here? But we agreed it was a bit too early, and continued walking.

Steve caught a glimpse of people up ahead. We could hear their voices and see their characteristic red light. These were the folks working on the maintenance of the abandoned station, or maybe on a part of another active station that had been shut off and put out of use. I'm not sure. We maneuvered ourselves some distance away from them but could see several workers. A dark shape perhaps fifty feet away called to someone else we couldn't see. I didn't hear what he said, but we had no doubt it was in regards to us. We decided to make a break for it to avoid any trouble.

After a while, we arrived at what must have been Canal Street Station. We were separated from the platform by only a single track. As long as no subway was coming, it was safe to cross. We glanced to the right, where a new train might come, but we didn't see anything. Steve, Andrew, Will, and I hopped over the electric-powered rails and crossed the tracks. A platform is much higher above the ground than you might think if you've only ever looked down from above. It took me more than a little effort to hoist myself up with my backpack on. But I made it on the first try and breathed a sigh of relief. The other three made it up at the same time.

We continued on, but when I turned I could see that Jacki and

Brent were still on the tracks. My mom's advice was well founded. Brent took off and jumped, throwing his body forward, but slid back down into the tracks. I turned and sprinted back to him. He still had all of his gear with him. It's strange what conscientious people choose to undertake even in a dangerous situation. I grabbed him and helped pull him up.

Jacki's head and the top of her chest barely reached platform. She was also carrying a backpack, making it extra difficult to get up. She clawed at the platform and tried without luck to scramble up. For a moment I gazed into her dark-brown eyes. She looked terrified, and for good reason. Jacki has worked as a war correspondent in some of the world's most dangerous, war-torn areas. Now, at home in New York standing down in the subway tracks knowing that a subway might come at any second was not a favorable notion.

Some passengers waiting on the platform stood looking at her, some chose to glance off in another direction. Maybe they didn't want to be involved in witnessing an accident. Brent and I each grabbed one of Jacki's shoulders and lifted her onto the platform. She stood up, and as we jogged from the station I met the gaze of a man standing in a suit and tie and wearing thick glasses. He turned away. I wondered what he must be thinking, to see a gang of adults suddenly appearing, hopping across the train tracks? Maybe he wished he could come with us rather than going home?

Safely out of the station, we decided to head to the next McDonald's for coffee and tea. I hadn't looked at my watch and had no idea how long we'd been underground. Next to us, a girl wearing a hoodie sat with the volume of her little ghetto blaster turned up. She had placed it on the table in front of her and was listening to Lady Gaga sing 'Born This Way.' I heard the final lines as I sat down: 'I'm on the right track, Baby/I was born this way, hey!' This was the area that Lady Gaga, or Stefani Joanne Angelina Germanotta, as she is named, lived in before she had her big break-through. My daughters and I all like Lady Gaga. I have tried to explain to them how I believe that the best, and maybe the worst, day of her life was when the record label, Def Jam, gave her the boot. It had paid her a sizable advance—life up to that point had been about becoming a big pop star, and now it seemed it was going to happen for her. But then the label regretted its decision and sent her packing. 'I went back to my apartment on the Lower East Side, and I was so depressed [...]. That's when I started the real devotion to my music and art.' On edge, depressed, but at about the same time there was a hard-nosed voice growing inside of her that said she was going to do this. 'I am going to get a new nose, and I'm moving to LA, and I'm going to be huge.' She bleached her hair and someone, maybe even she herself, started circulating rumors of substance abuse, wild partying, and, after a while, that she was a man. Gaga is among the stars who claim to be open about their cocaine abuse, but no one has ever seen her snorting a line of coke.

She became a better artist first and foremost due to the opposition she faced and to her tough-as-nails work ethic. 'One day, you're not going to go into a deli without hearing me,' she said to *New York Magazine* in 2010—and she was right. The best form of revenge, as we all know, is success. Of course she was happy, topping the charts with one number-one hit after another, but I somehow suspect that this was nothing compared to the feeling she got when she began to gain trust in herself and think, 'They should see me now!'

We dispersed soon afterward. There wasn't any point sitting and waiting for the police, who might be on the lookout for us. Brent and Jacki went to get some sleep. Will did, too, so it was just Steve, Andrew, and I left. With all the maintenance workers in the subway, we dropped our idea of sleeping in an abandoned station. It was still dark out, so we decided to climb up Williamsburg Bridge before dawn.

Steve suggested we pass by Canal Park at the Hudson River along the way. Our plan was to climb into the sewer at Canal Street the following night, and we wanted to be able to exit out of a manhole tunnel there. Since we were already in the neighborhood, it was a good idea to check whether the manhole cover was easy to open. We made our way in that direction. The park was enclosed by a picket fence. Andrew stood guard while Steve and I climbed across. There were some large manholes located in the north-western part of the park, and we sat down on a nearby bench. We chatted and shot the breeze for a few minutes, in case anyone from the surrounding buildings noticed us and wondered what we might be up to. Then we stood and sort of moseyed over toward one of the holes, leaned over, opened it up, and looked down. There was a nice stream flowing along down there. We replaced the cover and climbed back over the fence.

7. WILLIAMSBURG BRIDGE: THE USE OF CLIMBING MOUNT EVEREST

'The first question you will ask, and which I must try to answer, is this, "What is the use of climbing Mount Everest?" and my answer at once must be, "It is no use." There is not the slightest prospect of any gain whatsoever. Oh, we may learn a little about the behavior of the human body at high altitudes, and possibly medical men may turn our observation to some account for the purposes of aviation. But otherwise nothing will come of it. We shall not bring back a single bit of gold or silver, not a gem, nor any coal or iron. We shall not find a single foot of earth that can be planted with crops to raise food. It's no use. So, if you cannot understand that there is something in man which responds to the challenge of this mountain and goes out to meet it, that the struggle is the struggle of life itself, upward and forever upward, then you won't see why we go. What we get from this adventure is just sheer joy. And joy is, after all, the end of life. We do not live to eat and make money. We eat and make money to be able to live. That is what life means and what life is for.'

GEORGE MALLORY

George Mallory dreamed of reaching the summit of Everest up until his death. Reading his words above, I appreciate his honesty about how little importance most expeditions actually have.

Happiness doesn't last long on the summit of Everest, and a prerequisite of the joy that you feel up there is that the trip has been strenuous. Reaching the top by flying is not the same thing. It has to cost something in the form of hard work. It is the long journey that is exciting, not the winnings.

Mallory reminds us that, all in all, there is very little that we *must* do in our lives. If you decide to do something, it might go well; if you decide on not doing anything, it might also turn out to be okay. But achieving something too easily can quickly suck the joy out of

---

Mallory reminds us that, all in all, there is very little that we *must* do in our lives. If you decide to do something, it might go well; if you decide on not doing anything, it might also turn out to be okay. But achieving something too easily can quickly suck the joy out of it.

---

it. Happiness, struggle, and absurdity appear as three sides of the same thing. George Mallory died as he lived, on Everest in 1924. No one knows for certain whether he was on his way up or down from the summit. He had brought a photo of his wife Ruth along with him, who had written to him in many of her letters: 'I would rather grow old with you than anyone in the world. You have already made me into a better person.' He hoped to leave the photo at the summit. When his body was discovered, the photograph was not with him. Either he had left it at the top, or he had lost it, or he hadn't brought it along at all. The last option is so disappointingly unromantic that I disregard that possibility altogether.

Climbing to the top of a bridge across East River, as we were about to do, is of course something quite different than climbing up Mount Everest, but here, as well, it is more rewarding to look out over the view from the top when you've had to work to climb up yourself. It was about three in the morning on Wednesday, December 15th. Steve, Andrew, and I hoped to get down off the bridge before it got light, so in order to save time we hailed a taxi and asked the driver to drop us off at the western edge of the bridge. We got off at the end of the bridge, where Clinton Street starts.

The bridge was completed in 1903, and at the time was the world's longest suspension bridge. A steel tower stands at each convergence, holding the cables aloft. The bridge is around 6,600 feet across. Steve thought the whole thing looked bulky. Looking up at the construction, I thought it seemed to have been constructed with two goals: efficiency, and the ambition of being as big as possible. A classically inspired portal directly ahead of us at the start of the bridge reminded me somewhat of a European triumphal arch. Four lanes, train tracks, and a bike and pedestrian path led straight across toward Brooklyn and Queens. There was enough traffic that we decided not to risk walking on one of the cables to the top of the tower. If we were spotted by a policeman or a talkative taxi driver, we could end up being arrested. 'You know you're fucked,' Steve remarked, 'when there's suddenly no more traffic on the bridge. That means that the police have closed it off and are looking for you.'

The cables are equipped with suicide guards, large gates located a bit in front of the cables to keep suicidal people from jumping.. It seems strange that someone who has decided to kill him- or herself would be afraid to climb over a barrier like this, but that's how it is. We chose instead to reach the south-western tower by taking the bike and pedestrian path, which was enclosed in a red chain-link fence. The holes of the fence were small, making it difficult to climb over. The subway and cars thundered along below us, but there weren't any other pedestrians or bicyclists to be seen.

Along the riverbank were both a police station and a fire station built with red brick, almost like one of the classic forts of the Wild West with a little tower and an American flag fluttering at the top. I had never climbed a bridge before. It didn't seem too difficult. First, there was a large metal gate, strong and at least six feet high. I grabbed on, grasped the top of the gate and pulled myself over. I hoped this would be the only one, but when I looked ahead, I saw another gate. A bit higher up, and more exposed, in case I should fall.

I don't talk about it much, but I feel uneasy when I look down from great heights. When I climbed Everest, I concentrated deeply within myself to avoid vertigo. Here, I began to feel the old fears rising up. But this was neither the place nor the time for emotional reflections, as 'my ample theme impels me onward,' as Dante has it. I tried to look up and not down as I climbed the gate. I placed the front of my left foot in a hole in the fence, grabbed the top of the fence, and swung my leg around, followed by my entire body. For one moment, I quickly looked down from the top of the fence to the cars racing past thirty feet below, and to the river far down, but then I turned my gaze upward again.

On the other side of the fence, there was a metal staircase that led the rest of the way up. Very civilized. A fresh breeze was blowing and I clasped the railing as we continued our ascent. The tower protruded into the air about a three hundred feet over the East River, and when we had finally reached the top, the view left us breathless. We stood on a veranda-like platform made of steel or iron. To the west, we could see where we had just come from, Manhattan, and to the east we looked towards Brooklyn and Queens, where we were planning to go in the next days. I thought I could even see Coney Island in the distance. We were enjoying ourselves up there on top. Even though I had to hold onto the railing, I was first and foremost overwhelmed by the joy of seeing New York from this perspective. Andrew, Steve, and I hugged each other and stood looking out with our arms around one another for a few seconds.

Existentialism in Practice

From up high on the bridge, Manhattan looked like a long chain of mountains. To the south-west, we could make out the empty space where the World Trade Center used to be, and where the French balance artist, Phillipe Petit, walked a thin wire between the two towers, 1,368 feet above the ground, on the morning of August 7th, 1974. 'In a way, Petit is one of my heroes,' said Steve, 'but I didn't like the documentary about his feat, *Man on Wire*. It was too simple.' One of the messages in the film was Petit's habit of sacrificing friendships to realize his dreams, which Steve believed was speculative and incorrect. When Petit was finally arrested by the police, according to his own book, *To Reach the Clouds*, he was asked by a police officer whether he was resisting his arrest. Petit denied this, but replied: 'But I am resisting death.'

I can identify with this sentiment. It is existentialism in practice: to be present in the moment, and to give yourself the freedom to follow your dreams. To grasp at something that is outside of yourself. 'Life should be lived on the edge of life. You have to

---

If I were the president, I would use my commencement speech to encourage everyone to be thankful each time the sun rises, and to show gratitude for everything that it does for us. It is a good way to start off the day.

---

exercise rebellion,' says Petit in the film, with his characteristic heavy French accent. The choices that I take throughout are my own, and I alone am responsible for them. No one else is to blame. Life in the here and now is something meaningful. When Børge Ousland and I were charged by a polar bear close to the

North Pole and were forced to shoot it, the question on all of our minds was who is going to eat whom for lunch. When I was stuck hanging on a snow bridge as I walked alone to the South Pole, kicking with my legs hanging over a deep ice crevice, the past and future ceased to exist. Here in New York, I had many of the same feelings. Going on a journey is about recognizing that you are alive, and about being present in your own life. Philosophers write about existentialism, but life on an expedition is realized existentialism.

The journey through New York was about breaking down routine patterns. 'I was cleaning and, meandering about, approached the divan and couldn't remember whether or not I had dusted it,' wrote Leo Tolstoy in his diary. 'Since these movements are habitual and unconscious I could not remember and felt that it was impossible to remember.' He concluded that if he had dusted and couldn't remember it, and no one had seen it, then it was the same as if it hadn't happened. 'If the whole complex lives of many people go on unconsciously, then such lives are as if they had never been,' said Tolstoy. And this is how it is: when my daily life becomes routine, when everything has become habitual, it is as though I am not present in my life. I could just as well have been zeroed out. That's when it's high time to shake things up, don my backpack, and defy my own rules. To experience freedom by going against what is expected. To make new choices and decide for something that isn't certain. Stirring up habits can be as simple as choosing a new route to work or leaving home to walk underground through New York.

To the east, the sun still hovered below the horizon out in the Atlantic Ocean, but in the half hour that we stood at the top of the bridge, we could sense how the city was slowly lighted up before the sun was even visible. The sunlight would soon touch the top of the bridge and spread over the buildings opposite us, cautiously warming up the city. I felt my own joy at the idea. If I were the president, I would use my commencement speech to encourage everyone to be thankful each time the sun rises, and to show gratitude for everything that it does for us. It is a good way to start off the day.

We had to descend before we were seen. Our descent went quickly; we walked down the stairs and climbed back over the fences. It was Wednesday morning as we headed back toward Manhattan and to Essex Street Station. Before leaving the island once and for all, we planned on walking through the Westside Tunnel that stretched from around 125th Street down to Penn Station, as well as the sewer system around Canal Street. Despite what the song says, that the city never sleeps, it isn't quite true. Around us, everything was still and the streets were almost completely empty.

When the inhabitants are at home and the cars are all parked, it's easy to see how run-down the buildings are and all the garbage that lines the sidewalks. Walking along, we saw restaurants, shops selling cheap, brand-name clothing or rip-offs, and stores advertising bargain diamonds and good deals. It seemed like the pinnacle of optimism to believe that here, in precisely this location, there was an exception for the sale of precious stones.

Steve and I agreed to make our way north through the subway tunnel for a few dozen city blocks, past the large station beneath Union Square and 14th Street. We went down the stairs, scanned our Metro passes at the entryway, and stood on the platform. We peered into the tunnel. It was disappointing to see that there was maintenance work being done here as well. We turned and exited again. As we left, we met a maintenance worker and asked him what was going on. He explained that there was maintenance work all the way past Union Square. I wondered whether he understood what we were hoping to do and whether he suspected us. But he seemed so serious as he told us that I believed him.

Nowadays it seems that a serious facial expression is perceived as more sincere than a positive expression. 'I looked quite stern in the photograph because I think people will not trust me if I smile,' reasons Sophia in Alice Munro's short story 'Too Much Happiness.'

It was now completely light out. Andrew wanted to go home and rest. We said goodbye, and Steve and I decided to head up to the Westside Tunnel to find a spot to sleep. Steve looked tuckered, and I must have as well. Neither of us had slept since the previous day at Columbia. We hailed a taxi and rode to Riverside Park, around 120th Street. Nearby, we saw one of the US's largest cathedrals, the Cathedral of Saint John the Divine, where Petit was installed as a permanent artist after his rise to fame, and undertook to tightrope-walk on a line hung inside the church. Steve had climbed up the outer side of it. We walked north through a park and past some tennis courts until we arrived at a busy one-way road that led to Westside Highway, the freeway that follows along the west side of Manhattan.

I looked carefully up and down the street as we crossed over. Most accidents happen when one doesn't expect them. Safely across, we could make out the train tracks only about six feet away and below us. We clambered through bushes growing down toward the railroad, scaled a fence, jumped, and landed on the Amtrak railroad tracks heading north out of the city.

8. WESTSIDE TUNNEL, AKA FREEDOM TUNNEL, MANHATTAN

Everything was quiet, the tunnel was nice and wide, and we began our walk south. Of course, it wasn't really a tunnel, more of a superstructure. In the 1930s, labor and steel were cheap, and Robert Moses, who was a city planner and possibly one of the most powerful men in the city for five decades, decided (despite the fact that he had never been democratically elected) that a canopy would be constructed over the railway tracks that already existed there. Thus the inhabitants of the area, which at that time had relatively little means, were provided an opportunity to walk to the Hudson River without having to cross over the tracks. A nice thought, but shortly afterwards a measure was passed to construct a motorway next to the tunnel, which cut off the path of the inhabitants. Moses was a pioneer in creating busy roadways to divide neighborhoods, thus skirting accusations that he helped further racial and class segregation in the city.

Daylight filtered in through a grid in the ceiling overhead. The sun had returned, and this was something good to think about. The soft light lighted up long icicles hanging from the enormous steel girders holding up the roof. The apparently completely oversized structure was an impressive sight. We admired it by the light of our flashlights and the little bit of daylight that seeped in.

It had been in the Westside Tunnel that Steve and I had taken our first trial run in August. That's when we met Brooklyn, a woman who has lived in the tunnel since 1982. Just beyond her 'igloo,' which is what she called the cement space she lived in, twelve feet above the tracks, there were a few other places that would be ideal for setting up camp. We figured that she wouldn't be awake at this time of day and decided to try to catch some sleep in one of these spaces. Steve has known Brooklyn for many years and the last time we met her, she seemed healthy and fit. Her face and eyes had overflowed with happiness. And even though life as a homeless person was difficult, the dumpsters up on the street for the most part contained everything that a person needs of food, drink and clothing.

How Happy Are You, on a Scale of One to Ten?

Brooklyn's underground existence had begun twenty-eight years earlier, in the fall. She had been living in a park, where there were many cats she liked to feed. Later in the fall it got colder and, in the end, she had decided to go after the cats to see where they spent their nights. She followed them to the tunnel, where she discovered an enclosed space. She's lived there ever since. There were several settlements here in the 1990s. The 2000 documentary *Dark Days* portrays this area and the life in the tunnel from these days. Small houses had been erected in the tunnel and a somewhat organized society was formed. Since then, the authorities have captured and evicted most of the inhabitants, but they haven't been able to remove Brooklyn. She doesn't want to live anywhere else. She is a genuine individualist in a country that adores individualism—but just not her form of individualism. I wouldn't have dared to try getting her to leave.

When I am on travels, I often wonder how happy the people are who I come across. Most people seem pretty satisfied. When I met Brooklyn for the first time, I was curious about her thoughts on this topic. I asked if she could answer some questions about her own happiness, and she replied that this was no problem. 'How happy are you, on a scale of 1 to 10?' 'Seven,' she replied, and added, 'sometimes eight.' Brooklyn went on to explain that she is the happiest when she is playing with her cats and feeding them, and when she sings.

I have put this question to many people throughout the world, and almost everyone answers with the number seven, plus or minus. Once, when travelling east to Kamuli in Uganda with my daughters—Ingrid, Solveig, and Nor—we got to know a woman who lived with her seven children, hens, and her husband in a

---

There are two harvest seasons in Kamuli. The couple explained that they were happiest close to the harvests, especially if it proved to be a good year.

---

hut of about forty square feet. There were three beds in the hut, but no electricity nor water, and there wasn't even a bucket to use as a toilet. After thinking about my questions, she also answered seven, just as most Scandinavians do, but added thoughtfully that her happiness was closer to eight. Her husband maintained a straight seven. He had two wives and seventeen children between them.

There are two harvest seasons in Kamuli. The couple explained that they were happiest close to the harvests, especially if it proved to be a good year. The nice thing about travelling with your children is that they get to see the world with new eyes. After three days in Kamuli, my daughter Solveig remarked that it was strange how people here were so much more cheerful than most Norwegians, even though we are so rich and they are so poor.

We had promised Brooklyn to return. Steve had spoken to her later that fall, and she had told him that she was turning fifty in December. Steve had guaranteed that we would have a birthday party for her, and that I would bring a birthday cake. The idea was that we would celebrate this on the third day of our trip, on Wednesday evening. There were still twelve hours to go, and since there wasn't any sign that Brooklyn was awake yet, we decided to continue on.

It's easy to think of Brooklyn's life as unconventional and my own as normal. I often think of myself as the norm. But to think of my life in Norway, the world's richest country, where health care and education are free, and where the government expenditure on welfare is the highest per capita worldwide (with the exception of a few other oil capitals)—is this more normal than being a homeless pauper in a large city? The answer, of course, is no. I am unconventionally privileged. It is good to be reminded of this.

The tunnel walls were covered in graffiti, and with the filtered light that seeped through overhead air grids, it is a unique gallery for displaying art. Well-known painters such as Smith and his brother Sane (who died in 1991), COST, TWIST, GHOST, Freedom, and REVS have dominated the walls with their figurative paintings, but also with their distinctive forms of expressionism. Freedom's version of Goya's *The Third of May 1808* is possibly one of the most often-cited artworks from the end of the last century. Westside Tunnel is also called Freedom Tunnel, and some say that the name stems from the artist, while others claim it has to do with the freedom from not being seen, or the freedom not to pay rent.

Unfortunately, the Amtrak train service has its own agenda. The works of art barely have time to age before the maintenance workers come and spray over them with grey paint. Several of the paintings that we had admired in August had been painted over when we returned in December. It is a struggle between the authorities and the artists, but the authorities will never win. New artworks are painted, slowly and surely. REVS had been there earlier than us and had created several large pictures, but many of the classics that should be protected end up disappearing instead. What is called law and order on one day can easily be seen as vandalism on the next.

I hadn't noticed it earlier, but as we continued walking, I saw Steve pause, as if he were in pain. I asked whether he had hurt himself. 'No, I had a rare cancer in my hip, Gorham-Stout Syndrome, and it will never be the same again,' he answered. 'There's nothing like hanging out in a pediatric cancer ward to realize how lucky you actually are,' he continued with a smile, thereby formulating his own variation of the German philosopher Arthur Schopenhauer's view: 'Only pain and desire can really be felt [...]. Therefore, we don't even notice the three largest goods that life offers—good health, youth and freedom—as long as we possess them. It's only after we have lost them [...] we discover that we were happy when the unhappiness takes over.'

Many people had recommended that Steve take it easy, but the illness marked a turning point in his life. As the fridge magnet says, 'You only live once. But if you work it right, once is enough.' He had seen how fragile life is, and that it is important to make the most of it. I recognized myself in this. Not because I have had cancer, too, but because I try not to take life for granted and to see it instead as a gift. Any one of us could be hit by a bus tomorrow. Our existence is made richer, but also more sober, with this realization. 'How can you think yourself a great man, when the first accident that comes along can wipe you out completely?' asked the Greek dramatist Euripides. It's a good thing to keep in mind.

Remember My Prayer to You

It wasn't easy finding a place comfortable enough to sleep and hidden enough so that the train conductors and maintenance workers wouldn't see us. We ended up walking the entire way down to the area around 70th Street. The tunnel widened out and became more spacious. When we arrived, we decided to stop in to visit a man living in a small hole below the train tracks nearby. We had come by his place in August, but he hadn't been at home then.

WELCOME had been written in large letters on the trap door next to the tracks, which was his entrance. It was like a doormat. We knocked but didn't receive any answer. We knocked again, and Steve called out that it was he, and that we just wanted to chat. They knew each other. But there still wasn't any answer. We opened the door slightly and looked down. The light was on—electricity is 'free' in this area, and all of these people just hook up to the network by hand. The last time we had looked in, the place had been neat and organized. This time, the area of barely ten square feet was in disarray.

We replaced the door and I looked at Steve. He seemed about to cry. He loved the people here; he respected them and the lives that they lived. And he thought it was sad that society couldn't accept that some people chose to live a life other than what was expected. Of course we have to be cautious about romanticizing life in a train tunnel, beneath the tracks where both goods and passenger trains pass, and against the wishes of the authorities. But when the alternatives are shelters, or night hospitals, I believe that life down here is much better. Spending nights in shelters can be brutal, with robbery, heavy drug dealing, intimidation, and theft. And in the morning you have to gather your belongings quickly and get out again.

Steve was annoyed that he couldn't remember the man's name. It was important to him, but he had forgotten it. In a circle of hell just below the level that houses Helen, Cleopatra, and Achilles, a tortured soul tells Dante, 'But when you walk once more where life is sweet, bring me, I beg, to others in remembrance. No more I'll say, nor answer any more,' and then he enters into a kind of trance. In Dante's work, as in New York, anonymity is a type of punishment. In a way, we both felt that we owed it to the man to talk about him with his real name, and that someone should remember him now that he had possibly passed on for good. The man had been abandoned to that which I believe Marlow touches on in *Heart of Darkness* as, 'that oblivion which is the last word of our common fate.'

We returned to the place we'd decided we would sleep, a bit more than 100 feet from the tracks and obscure enough that no one would see us unless they were searching. It was about ten o'clock in the morning, and it had been a long day and night. We rolled out our sleeping mats and bags and settled down.

As I lay there, I thought about how delightful it is to be able to crawl into a sleeping bag whenever and wherever you want. To have everything that you need in your backpack. To make do with that, and only that. Not to have to take responsibility for anyone else, and not to be dependent on having to arrive at a certain place at the end of each day. We might be on our journey for four days, maybe seven. I wore the same clothes the entire time: blue corduroy pants, one short and one long pair of underpants, woolen long underwear, and a blue checked cotton shirt. I never removed the long underwear for the entire duration of the trip.

It was cold. I had only brought a light sleeping bag to spare the weight. One hour after we lay down, I woke up freezing. I was still wearing my long underwear. My pants lay under my head as a pillow. We were spread out on cement and there was a chilly draught in the air. I squirmed in my sleeping bag. It had been such a long time since I had lain freezing out in the wild that I had forgotten what it was like. Now the cold had already settled in my body. It was an interesting feeling, because the most tempting option, that

Home to the city's 'unseen citizens.' The entryway is discreet: a metal sheet on the floor with a greeting painted on it. This place of residence is in the Westside Tunnel, one yard away from and under the freight and passenger train tracks that run north out of the city.

Steve checks if anyone is at home, but it seems abandoned.

The living quarters are about twenty square feet and contain a bed, oven, digital clock, and small radio.

of remaining in the sleeping bag and freezing—wasn't realistic. I got up, climbed halfway out, froze some more, waved my arms, took out my bubble jacket and laid it on top of myself. Back in my sleeping bag, I continued massaging those parts of my body that were cold. The warmth slowly returned and I slept again.

It was four in the afternoon when we woke. We had overslept. Before falling asleep, my plan had been to surprise Steve with a cup of warm tea while he was still in his sleeping bag, but now there was nothing but to get up and get going. We were supposed to make it through the rest of the tunnel, almost forty blocks, to Penn Station, where we would buy a cake and brandy for Brooklyn's birthday. We drank some water and ate a few nuts. Steve relieved himself in the corner, and then we left. We saw a tunnel resident ahead of us. He moved heavily, his head down and covered with his hood, almost blending into his surroundings. He barely lifted his feet from the ground but dragged his knees across and down for each step. A type of moonwalk. We sped up and reached him, saying hello. The man didn't even lift his head, and continued in the same calm tempo before disappearing.

He was one of the city's invisible people.

The 1952 novel *Invisible Man* is about an inhabitant who is like air to everyone else. Ralph Ellison wrote it halfway through his life. The main character, whose name we never learn, is pulled into society's underworld and settles illegally in a Harlem cellar. 'I am an invisible man,' he says to describe himself. Not invisible in the sense of ghost stories; he is invisible because he is black and therefore no one takes notice of him. He ceases in a way to be an individual, and is like vapor in his surroundings. The only entity who cares about his existence for a while is the electricity provider, which registers that someone is stealing electricity, though they never find him in the cellar. Ellison describes Harlem, black

America's capital, as a place of hope and dreams but also of despondency.

'I was a nigger for twenty-three years. I gave that shit up. No room for advancement,' quips one of my favorite comedians, Richard Pryor.

We stood and looked in the direction in which the man had vanished, but he was gone for good, and we continued walking south through the tunnel. Every now and then a train passed and we had to hide. The tunnel was wide and tall, and when the trains came we crouched together along the wall away from the trains or behind a bump in the concrete so as not to alarm the conductor. The trains seemed to run on half-hour schedules. Two trains into the city and two trains out of the city per hour, plus freight trains. The tunnel was wide and straight, but it wasn't always covered, so that sometimes we would emerge out into the open sky where we would gaze up to the surrounding skyscrapers. For the most part they were new buildings, as far as I could tell—built to meet the demand for homes and office spaces, which optimists believe will never end. It was late on Wednesday afternoon. Dusk was falling across the city and the moon had once again become visible. I have always been captivated by the moon. Every time I see it, it looks a bit different where it sits 240,000 miles above my head. The light that it casts over the earth is like a quiet reflection, large and mild. It comes from so far away, in contrast to all the other lights in New York, and seems more friendly and welcoming. The moon has been to me like a steadfast friend who reappears after bad weather, in the polar nights, at home, or as on this night as I emerged, sluggish and squalid, from the tunnel where I had been sleeping.

I looked at Steve, who was walking ahead of me. The moonlight had rendered his form a nearly imperceptible silhouette

One of New York's best-known artworks: Freedom's version of Goya's *The Third of May 1808*. Authorities painted over the artwork shortly after this photo was taken.

José made his home on the ground at the end of this side track. Nearby is where his friend was hit by a morning train.

against the railway tracks. The shadows from moonlight are different than the sharp shadows cast by the bright light of the sun, or by a lamp. I watched the moon as I walked until we came to the next tunnel, and I had the feeling that all light comes down from above and all darkness comes up from the earth.

Back underground, around 40th Street, we searched for José. He is a veteran who has lived in this area for many years. Steve and I met him in August during our first, brief trip. Deep within a small corner of the tunnel, a bit away from the tracks, we first found him tucked into his sleeping bag with even the top opening shut to keep out the persistent flies. The flies here bite. It doesn't hurt so much, but it itches and can be irritating. In José's situation, the principles of deep ecology—that every creature has a positive impact—seem meaningless.

It appeared as though José had done little to make his domicile cozier since we last met him. A mattress had been laid down in a short side tunnel where no trains ran, and various objects had been strewn around him: blankets, a jacket, a sweater, a few other garments, some old newspapers, and a suitcase. José is a likeable, low-key guy. Small, compact, and resilient. It's a good workout walking around searching for empty bottles, cans, food in dumpsters, and more.

I put the same questions to him that I had posed to Brooklyn: how happy was he? He also answered seven, but after a while, he said that actually it was more like a three. That's what happens. 'Ask yourself whether you are happy, and you cease to be so,' wrote the British philosopher John Stuart Mill. But José's life had been brutal. Last winter, he and his neighbor—a man living a short jog up the tracks in the tunnel, where he had a nice view out over the tracks and a blue sofa and a bed—had been sitting, each on their own track, drinking heavily. It was after the last train had passed, so they were feeling safe. Both had become so drunk that they fell asleep. His companion had apparently fallen over backward and slept with his legs stretched out on the tracks when the morning train came. He was cut into three, but José said that he was still alive after that. The entire tunnel was closed off, rescue crews and ambulances arrived, and his buddy was taken to the hospital. The authorities had since attempted to chase José out of the tunnels, and he had been harassed by a gang of youths who had lighted his things on fire. I inquired how his friend was doing now. José answered that when his friend never returned after three weeks, he supposed he must have died. His bed and sofa still remained farther up in the tunnel, but José had assumed ownership of his glasses and a few dollars that had been left over.

Now, a few months later, José was also gone. We found the place where he had lived, but there were only a few scattered relics: the mattress, a blanket or two, and some discarded belongings that had become trash. Or maybe they had been trash the entire time. It might even have seemed like he hadn't taken anything with him when he had departed for the last time.

The Hunt for Birthday Cake

There was an opening close to 30th Street where the tunnel dove again for its last stretch before the final station. We didn't want to risk being seen and decided to exit the tunnel here. This was easier said than done, however, as enormous barbed-wire fences had been erected along the tracks. The barbed wire lay piled in spirals atop each other. Fortunately, we were wearing good gloves and thick clothing, and even new barbed-wire fences have weaknesses if you look for them. We located a post where it was easier to climb up the fence. It was simple getting to the top of the fence, but the part after that, before the body's full weight had shifted to the other side and you could jump down, was a bit unnerving. You had to be concentrated and keep your balance so as not to get stuck in the barbs.

We sauntered east, up through the city. Steve and I popped into a little restaurant and ordered sushi. As we sat eating, I received a text message from Alan. He had decided to join us after all. I had sent him an email earlier inviting him back. Jacki and Brent also wanted to join the birthday party. This was nice. We wanted to hold a big celebration for Brooklyn, and in this case it would be great to have a lot of people. Steve also sent around an invitation to a few of his friends. Now it was time for us to find a real birthday cake. Steve and I split up and agreed to meet at Tom's Restaurant two hours later. I began walking along the street on my search, asking passers-by where I might find a good bakery, but it seemed as if birthday cakes had gone out of fashion in New York. I felt a bit groggy. There had been several changes in my internal clock in the last days. First the difference between Norwegian and New York time, and now our own expedition time. I ambled up and down streets, searching, but couldn't find the cake I'd been envisioning. I had to settle for something more ordinary instead. I was annoyed. Generic cakes are no good if one is celebrating a big birthday.

In my backpack, however, I had the chocolate that my daughter, Nor, had made for Brooklyn's birthday. She had originally made the chocolate for her friends, but had changed her mind when she'd heard about the fiftieth-birthday party. One of Socrates' fundamental ideas was that doing good deeds can make you happier, and that you therefore benefit from behaving well. It seems obvious, but is nonetheless difficult to live up to. The Chinese philosopher, Confucius, who lived around the same time as Buddha and Socrates, maintained something similar: you must be able to do 'something for nothing'; that is, if you wish to be happy, you should act irrespective of the benefits that your acts may bring to you. What Buddha, Socrates, and Confucius are actually saying is that one of the most egotistical things that you can do is to help others. If your action is to help, this is fine, but almost regardless of the outcome, you will still most likely feel better by acting kindly.

After I'd already bought a dessert, I passed a shop that sold real cream cakes. Damn, was I happy, and I bought a big cake. Now all we had to do was to transport it safely up to 125th Street, over the fence, through the tunnel to 100th Street, and up to Brooklyn's igloo, all without damaging it.

9. AROUND 100TH STREET, MANHATTAN: BIRTHDAY WITH BROOKLYN

It was a large, strange party. Brooklyn was happy that we came. 'Hi! Welcome! Welcome to my igloo! Oh, you brought me a birthday cake! You remembered. That's nice! Let me see if it is ...' She checked to see that it was still in one piece. It nearly was. Then I presented her with the nicely packaged chocolate that Nor had made for her at home in my kitchen. Brooklyn was moved and glad.

Her home is difficult to reach. As I mentioned earlier, it is located about twelve feet above the tracks where she has a kind of terrace with a view out over the tunnel. To enter, we had to climb a staircase and creep through two small passageways. I had to remove quite a bit of clothing before I was small enough to squeeze through. Inside, propped against the wall, was a large poster of Lance Armstrong in a yellow jersey. Her bed was a mattress on the floor, nicely made up. A pile of empty bottles and cans comprising the bulk of her possessions were in the corner. A magazine article with photos of Michael Jackson had been torn out and the pages hung side by side on the wall. She also had a photo of herself looking very beautiful. Her home was simple, personal, and a bit draughty, with walls and roof made of concrete.

Everyone had brought drinks along, and pretty soon the bottles were being passed around. Just like at any Norwegian town party, there was cheering as someone brought out a bottle of liquor. I put the bottle of Redemption Rye Whiskey to my lips. Everyone drank from the same bottle. Andrew, who had joined us again, wanted to interview Brooklyn before the party took off. It was a bit of an odd seance, with the birthday girl as an object in the middle and the rest of us surrounding her as audience and interviewers. The celebration continued, but it was worth it, even though we actually needed rest much more than a party.

'It's called "appreciate what you got." And hold onto it. And don't lose it. I don't know why people are miserable—they got everything that I don't have. And I'm happier than them … I believe "treasure what you got,"' answered Brooklyn when I asked if she thought she was happier than those living above ground.

In a way, she has grasped the commercial principle responsible for the enormous growth in popular psychology and pharmaceuticals: we humans are never satisfied.

She continued, 'Because you never know when you're going to be in my place. A woman would be suicidal. She wouldn't even last a week down here. The second day, she going to learn how to appreciate her husband, her kids, and her house. And pay that rent. If you can survive here—you're like Frank. You can make it anywhere. But I'm quite sure Frank Sinatra didn't live down here.'

In a way, she has grasped the commercial principle responsible for the enormous growth in popular psychology and pharmaceuticals: we humans are never satisfied.

In addition, she has internalized an important concept of Buddha's teachings, and the third of his Four Noble Truths, that you will never achieve happiness if you do not conquer your own cravings and accept that they can never lead to satisfaction: 'To eliminate suffering, eliminate craving.' According to Buddha, happiness is something different and larger than material assets and emotional states of being. The first Noble Truth is that suffering exists, and the second is that the source of suffering is craving, or desire. The fourth provides steps for ending suffering, with the goal of nirvana, where one may obtain eternal peace and happiness.

Though she didn't have much, Brooklyn seemed thankful for what she did have. Two of our cultural heroes, Bart Simpson and Hamlet, offer yet another perspective. When asked to give thanks at the family dinner table, Bart bows his head and prays, 'Dear God, we paid for all this stuff ourselves, so thanks for nothing.' Being thankful is key to being content, but it's never been easy. Aristotle doesn't mention thankfulness, and Hamlet says, like Bart: 'I am even poor in thanks.'

Brooklyn mentioned a few times that we should probably go before her boyfriend B.K. came home, because he was 'really antisocial.' But she never mentioned when he might arrive, and suddenly he was there. And he was pissed. B.K.'s screamed hoarsely with his deep voice and she yelled back, trying to explain who we were. We could only see his silhouette in the dark corner. There was a lot of loud yelling back and forth. I heard Brooklyn scream something about a gun. Her boyfriend roared, and I couldn't make out most of what he said. Obviously, he wanted us to leave. We retreated through the two passageways and camped out on the other side. I can respect people who don't wish to be disturbed in their homes. Especially when there's mention of guns.

The party continued, and Brooklyn joined us a bit later. Her boyfriend had left to lie down at his own place, a bit further away from Brooklyn's igloo. There was drinking, smoking, and singing. From far down the tunnel we saw a light from someone at work. We were a bit worried they might report us, but the party had taken on a life of its own now, and there was no stopping it. Brooklyn sang, several of Steve's urban explorer pals arrived, and Will, Will's cousin, Moses, and everyone else got buzzed. It developed into a round of singing. Brooklyn led off, and from what

I could make out, the songs she started with were first and foremost hits from the time before she had lived in the tunnel: 'We Are Family,' 'Ain't No Mountain High Enough,' and so on. ''Cause baby,/There ain't no mountain high enough/Ain't no valley low enough/Ain't no river wide enough/To keep me from getting to you.' She had a terrific voice. And she was a terrific woman and looked me straight in the eyes as she sang it. I have always liked those lyrics.

Plato's Allegory of the Cave, in Reverse

I rolled out my sleeping bag and was about to nod off when Brooklyn lay down on top of me and gave me a goodnight kiss, with tongue and everything. Steve called over to Brooklyn that I had both children and a girlfriend, and she shook her head, laughed, and said, 'I don't want to get involved' as she got up. The racket continued, but my thoughts were somewhere else, even if I was three sheets to the wind. It had taken me so long to come to the same realizations that she had seemed to arrive at so easily. In a strange way, Brooklyn had intuited the teachings of the Stoics: the most important condition for happiness is accepting life's realities.

Seneca the Younger, the Roman philosopher, statesman, and one of the central Stoics, was subjected to much injustice. He was exiled to Corsica after being falsely accused of sexual relations with the emperor's niece. It was illegal at the time. When he was permitted to return to Rome, he began wondering why innocent people must experience so many terrible things. If life on earth is so unjust, how can anyone hope to be happy? It is the same question that Job poses in the *Bible*. Seneca didn't relent until he arrived at a firm answer: one must differentiate between those things that you can do something about and those about which you cannot do anything.

Seneca understood, as did Job and Brooklyn, that he must put the injustices behind him and accept that they had occurred if he ever wished to be happy. He chose to look ahead and concentrate on his future opportunities.

Another leading Stoic, the emperor Marcus Aurelius, asked himself whether the experience of happiness was more like dancing or wrestling. He believed it was more like wrestling, because happiness is about 'stand[ing] prepared and unshaken to meet what comes and what we did not foresee.'

I can't recall if Dante met any Stoics on his journey through hell. Maybe because none of them were there? However, just after exiting the underworld, at the entrance to purgatory, he meets the Stoic Cato the Younger. Cato had suffered defeat against Julius Caesar. They were both in constant battle, and in 46 B.C. he chose to commit suicide. He preferred death to dependence on Caesar's forgiveness. I am fascinated that someone could choose freedom in the form of death above allowing himself to be humbled. Cato stood at the entrance of purgatory to greet dead souls as Dante and Virgil arrived, but Virgil said to Cato: 'This man had yet to see his final evening; but, through his folly, little time was left before he did—he was so close to it. [...] He goes in search of liberty—so precious, as he who gives his life for it must know.'

Maybe I was too tipsy and naive to clearly perceive life in the tunnels on that evening, but I thought that despite everything, Brooklyn was better off than many above ground, and that she had achieved a deeper insight into human nature than most people who lived up there in civilization. It was a 180-degree shift of Plato's allegory of the cave: reality existed here below ground, while up above, people were living in an illusion.

Later that night, half asleep, I could hear many people rolling out their sleeping bags around me. We had agreed not to get up too late, and I set my alarm before going to sleep. When it went off at nine, Will, his cousin, and Moses were already gone. They had left for work. They had come all the way from Brooklyn late the previous night, had partied with us, and now they had gone directly to work. You've gotta respect that.

A day-after haze hung about the tunnel, and Liz, Alan, Andrew, and Steve looked drowsy from where they peered out of their sleeping bags. Empty bottles and trash lay discarded around us and barely anyone spoke. I could hear Brooklyn's voice from her igloo a ways away. She was humming a newer hit, 'Empire State of Mind,' which is performed by two of New York's natives, Jay-Z and Alicia Keys. Jay-Z has fought his way up in the opposite direction of Brooklyn: from poverty in New York to being a superstar. From what I could remember, Moses had convinced Brooklyn to sing the song just before I'd fallen asleep: 'New York, concrete jungle where dreams are made, oh/There's nothing you can't do/Now you're in New York/These streets will make you feel brand new.'

Little by little, we crept out from our cozy cocoons into the morning chill and headed north. Steve and I chatted while we walked. We were both a bit hung-over. A cold draught blew through the tunnels and the morning light sifted in through the ventilation grilles above us. He asked if I was still interested in trying out the sewer at Canal Street. I was, of course, but this was one stage we'd have to do by night. There was too much traffic in SoHo during the day. And anyway, we were in need of new waders. Since we hadn't passed through any water tunnels yet, we decided to use the day acquiring new waders and travelling north-east out of Manhattan toward Queens, where we'd heard tell of some lovely tunnels at Kissena Park and Underhill Avenue.

10. KISSENA PARK, QUEENS: HAPPINESS SEEMS OVERRATED

Having driven to the birthday party the previous night, Andrew now offered Steve, Liz, Alan, and me a ride to Orvis on Fifth Avenue, the city's most beloved store for fishing equipment. Though neither of us wanted to spend a lot of money on waders, it was the only place either Steve or I knew of that had waders in stock. The traffic was sluggish down from Harlem. We were crammed into the small car, which wasn't meant to seat five adults comfortably. Andrew offered to take a parallel street, but Steve and I both insisted on going down Fifth. We wanted to take in the most audacious contrasts each time we surfaced. First, we drove the Museum Mile. Posters outside the Jewish Museum announced an exhibition about Harry Houdini, the master escape artist and movie-star hopeful who also set the record for the quickest run around Central Park. Then we rode past The Metropolitan Museum of Art, where artifacts from excavation digs of old cities are on display and loading trucks are parked along the street. Perhaps someday the Met will exhibit findings from the developments of the last century in New York's underground?

We continued on, past the Frick Collection and the Guggenheim, named for two families who might now have been forgotten if they hadn't had museums named after them. People usually like to leave something behind, preferably something positive to make their lives seem more meaningful. This is especially evident in New York, with a number of references to dead people inside and outside of the city. Or, as Stephanie Savage, the co-creator of the New York *Gossip Girl* television series, put it: 'No one wants to die and discover that all you have to pass on to the next generation is your Facebook page.'

Fifth Avenue brims with wealth. After passing the museums, the street transformed into the ultimate shopping street. At this time of year, it was also the absolute Christmas jungle. Multi-storied buildings lined the streets, the sidewalks were crammed with stalls offering cheap rip-offs of handbags and wallets from the nearby shops, and around us on all sides the traffic inched forward. This is where the city's wealthiest inhabitants make their purchases, but also the thousands of tourists who come to New York for Christmas shopping. Normal people have to go elsewhere to check off their wish lists. As we drove past Bergdorf Goodman, I saw a woman coming out with two large shopping bags. She seemed gloriously happy. I could feel myself becoming happy just by looking at her. That paradise-like feeling most likely won't last, but whoever has said that money can't buy happiness was wrong.

Some Unromantic Considerations

Jesus, the Civil War, and the Titanic must be three of the most talked-about topics of all time in the USA. I've watched the film *Titanic* together with my daughters a number of times. The ship is the hero of the story as it sets sail on the sea for its virgin voyage, but the scene I remember best is when Kate Winslet makes a vow of lifelong love to Leonardo DiCaprio. She is willing to cast aside her life of luxury for him. The Slovenian philosopher Slavoj Žižek has addressed this moment of the film to ask whether it is really about a ship that sinks after crashing into an iceberg, a collision that 'takes place when the young lovers, immediately after consummating their relationship, return to the ship's deck.' Of even more importance is when Kate Winslet, whom Žižek compares to a kind of vampire who exploits a poor boy in order to discover herself, 'tells her lover that when the ship reaches New York the next morning, she will leave with him, preferring a life of poverty with her true love to a false, corrupted life among the rich.'

It is in this moment that the ship hits the iceberg, thereby preventing what would undoubtedly have been the true catastrophe, namely—according to the philosopher—their life together in New York. The stark reality of everyday life would most likely have destroyed their love. Žižek claims that the catastrophe intervenes in order to preserve their love, to uphold the illusion that if the ship hadn't gone down, they would have lived happily ever after: 'A further clue is provided by DiCaprio's final moments. He is freezing in the cold water, dying, while Winslet is safely floating on a large piece of wood. Aware that she is losing him, she cries: "I'll never let go!"— and as she says this, she pushes him away with her hands.'

Each time we watch the film, the entire Kagge household wishes that both of them could have lived out their lives happily. But Žižek was right: the film ends shortly after the moment we spectators assume is the happiest one in the characters' lives.

Kate Winslet probably would never have voluntarily given up a life along Fifth Avenue. If you've experienced both wealth and poverty, you prefer the first. I peered out at the city's largest toy store, FAO Schwarz, just behind the Apple Store inside a glass cube. Sometimes I get the impression that we have come a long way, historically speaking, in our consumer-driven society. But then I think about the relative newborn, Apple, and how quickly it has spread and propagated, and then I think that we are only in the Middle Ages of shopping. There will only continue to be more and more. We continued along the street. Louis Vuitton, Gucci, and Playboy Enterprises. There were Santa Clauses, decorations, and neon lights outside all of the car's windows. Wild and mesmerizing madness.

Arthur Schopenhauer, the philosopher who generally asserted that we are living in the worst of all imaginable worlds and that happiness is an illusion, understood already two hundred years ago something that psychologists understand about shopping: 'Through ownership of things, or the knowledge that we will own something, our demands increase, and this in turn increases our capacity to own more and demand more.' In a further aphorism, Schopenhauer argues that as soon as you reach the object of your desire, you realize how empty it is.

The joy of shopping peaks at the beginning of the experience and subsides with each further act of consumption. This is what is well known in economics as the 'law of diminishing marginal utility.'

Personally, I enjoy shopping, especially for art, but I also wholeheartedly agree with the old adage that the gift to be simple is the gift to be free. When Socrates witnessed a trove of jewels and other costly artifacts paraded through his city, he exclaimed: 'Good heavens, so many things that I wouldn't like to have.' I suspect he would have said something similar if he could have seen the array of goods on offer along Fifth Avenue.

We said goodbye to Andrew and entered Orvis. The store was full of shop-happy people. We were offered assistance. The clerk asked us what we planned to use our waders for. We told him. He thought for a moment before he asked whether there weren't crocodiles or other animals down there. This is a question we received quite often on our trip. My impression is that New York's inhabitants are willing to believe anything about what goes on underground. We assured him that the sewers were free of crocodiles and he offered useful advice about which waders to select. Once we'd each chosen our special-offer wading pants, the clerk began packing them gingerly into a bag, but Steve and I insisted this wouldn't be necessary.

We decided to rent a Zipcar for a few hours to get out to Kissena Park for our next underground tour. Steve's girlfriend Liz came along, as did Alan. On our way out of Manhattan, we passed by the New York Public Library on 42nd Street. A stronghold of knowledge in neoclassical style, built of white marble with columns, guarded by stone lions and stuffed full with millions of books. Anyone who wants to can go in, sit down, and read. Of all the buildings we'd seen, this was the one that emanated the most power. Maybe it was there, among the books, that I should be seeking answers to all my questions?

I'd already tried before to escape from the real world by delving deeply into the world of books, and I don't doubt that the answers to almost every question can be found among pages. I like reading, but I found that experience is the best teaching for me, even if it's costly.

We continued east toward Queens and passed by the city jail, Rikers Island. I always get melancholy when I see a prison and think of everyone within its walls. Guilty or not guilty. Minorities and the mentally ill are over-represented. In general, I think there are too many people under lock and key, and in the US, especially—around two million. The corrections industry is one of the branches that has continued to grow regardless of the country's economic situation. As long as the lawmakers keep lowering the threshold for what counts as an offence and increasing penalties, there's no reason to believe this growth will ever end.

Our stomachs were nearly on empty, and we drove to a gas station for nuts and water. I stood looking at the cover of *Cosmopolitan*. It almost felt like the magazine's messages had pursued me throughout the city: forever thin in January, perfect summer sex in June, more beautiful skin and a great love life all year long. Loyal readers are won by the precondition that none of the advice actually works.

Another world waits beneath most manhole covers.

The only action needed to escape from the everyday is to climb down a twelve-foot ladder.

I paid for the water and nuts and walked back to the car. We were all in a good mood as we drove east. Alan was happy to join us again, and I was growing to like Steve more and more. 'I'm fascinated by the lack of curiosity people have for the underground,' he said, 'especially because everything's based on it.' He continued: 'People have to realize they're part of an interactive ecology.' New York's inhabitants mostly look outward and upward.

Liz and Steve held hands while Liz drove. Alan and I sat in back. They didn't have to say much to communicate that they were in love. She had downloaded some of Steve's favorite songs and we listened to Avett Brothers' 'Love Like The Movies': 'Now in the movies they make it look so perfect/And in the background they're/Always playing the right song/And in the ending there's always a resolution/But real life is more than just two hours long.'

Liz had studied literature and gave me a tip for a poem to include in *Poems for Boys*, a new edition of an anthology I was planning to edit when I returned home: Frank O'Hara's 'Having A Coke With You.' As she quoted the poem, I knew immediately that I wanted to include it:

> *I look*
> *at you and I would rather look at you than all the portraits in the world*
> *except possibly for the* Polish Rider *occasionally and anyway it's in the Frick*
> *which thank heavens you haven't gone to yet so we can go together for the first time.*

Pleasure's Disloyal Cousin

The idea that Dante asserts in *The Divine Comedy*, that hell and paradise are polar opposites, doesn't always add up. In any case, I can't always manage to see the difference between paradise and hell, happy and unhappy moments. All four of us were looking forward to returning to our adventures in the sewers, where happiness consists of excrement and bad air in a confined tunnel.

The contrasting sensations comprise a whole that is not divisible, like frost and warmth. Comfort has a disloyal cousin called discomfort and the combination of the two produces happiness, and you can't separate them.

Moments of happiness, of course, require that one recognizes the alternative: in order to appreciate warmth, you have to know what it's like to freeze, so that next time I look out across Central Park and am warm and cozy, I'll be extra glad when I come back one day and am standing around shivering outside, a crowbar in hand.

But recently I'd begun to recognize something else. Happiness and well-being seemed to me misunderstood and overrated. Dante's and Freud's ideas that happiness and unhappiness were opposites didn't always seem to be the case. Sometimes it feels better to struggle at a task, to have sleepless nights, or to freeze than to relax and take pleasure in comfort.

One of the reasons I like to ski to the North Pole or look forward to jumping down a manhole is because happiness is somehow connected to that which is painful and repugnant; they both exist simultaneously, in the tunnel, or far out on the ice, or up near the top of Everest. The contrasting sensations comprise a whole that is not divisible, like frost and warmth. Comfort has a disloyal cousin called discomfort and the combination of the two produces happiness, and you can't separate them.

If you're wondering whether I think you should seek out scenarios in order to experience displeasure, my answer is no. As a baby, our first daughter Nor had terrible stomach pains and screamed herself to sleep, and screamed again when she woke up shortly thereafter. It was undoubtedly unpleasant for Nor, but when I think back on it, I realize that those months were more challenging for me than skiing to the South Pole. Still, I am glad in retrospect to have been present then, even if I would have done almost anything at the time to stop her stomach pains and the screaming. Because that was also such a rich time. That's the time it began to occur to me that happiness and unhappiness aren't necessarily opposites. On the contrary.

Some of the largest pleasures in life are often mirrored in hardship. Having children is demanding, keeping a house in order is, too, and there is almost always some challenge at work that I would choose to eliminate if I could. As a father and an employer, I know that it's possible to be irritated over problems in getting the ball rolling each day with kids and work, and at the same time to enjoy the same children and the same work. It's not so easy just to stop each day to reflect whether these may be the happiest days of my life. And I haven't really been motivated to do that either, mostly because there are so many other things to think about from day to day.

People usually cite memorable days as happy days. Like the birth of children, celebrations, and such. But many people are merely glossing over the truth when they claim these are their happiest days. It sounds so good and proper to say that the happiest day of my life was when I became a father or got married. And it may be true for many people. But my experience is that it's not easy to become happy on command. A funeral can be something positive, and a Christmas celebration something depressing. When Barack Obama was informed that he had won the Nobel Peace Prize, something that should have been good news for him, his first comment was, 'Oh, shit!'

Then there are other experiences—things that I wouldn't expect, often seemingly completely banal—that stick with me as moments of happiness. Like when Nor ran to me with outstretched arms after visiting the dentist for the first time, or when I found out, long after she'd been conceived, that I was going to be a father. Compared to these joys, the planned-out, immediate happiness that's marketed on posters and in life above ground seems completely to miss the mark.

A Shepherd's Life

A friend of mine who also likes walking is Fernando García-Dory, a shepherd. The shepherd culture in Europe is under threat nowadays, and so for the past years, he's tried to preserve the vocation by educating and training shepherds. One of the finest treks he knows of is when the sheep are herded through Spain from north to south or vice versa, depending on the season. The trek takes two months to complete. Like me, Fernando is interested in how different cultures create differing needs. One evening he sat shooting the breeze with a colleague about their joys in life, and the other shepherd told him: 'When you go walking with the sheep, and you see they walk, they run, they eat what they like, they keep moving, free, getting healthier, stronger. You see the lambs getting fatter. When you see the flock happy then, even when you make the camp every night, tired after many miles of walking, you also feel good, happy, and incredibly more relaxed.'

Fernando has accompanied many different nomadic people on journeys throughout the world. For Tuaregs, Berber nomads of the Sahara, happiness is found at the next oasis. For them, there is no difference between their desire and the goal of their profession. Fernando has posed the same question to everyone who crosses his path: 'Imagine you close your eyes and open them again in twenty years. What would make you happy to see?'

The answers are similar, whether among the Samburu or the Maasai from Tanzania or various tribes of Rajasthan. Everyone thinks that what would make them happiest is to see their flocks healthy and fat. They imagine families together, relaxing and enjoying nature, which would be rich and fertile. 'That's the harmony,' says Fernando, 'for those who wish to live in balance with nature. Instead of focusing on their individual needs, they look after the common needs, the ones of the community, in its expanded sense. From a son to a tree to a sheep.'

Though I don't wish to live as a shepherd, I think I would like to learn from them about presence and empathy.

The Common Thread

Liz parked the car at 164th Street and Underhill Avenue, near Kissena Park. It was ten past five on Thursday evening. There was a light drizzle, but not enough to make flooding a concern. The bad weather meant that there weren't many people out.

Liz, Alan, Steve, and I wanted to avoid drawing attention to ourselves, so we stole into the park to look for a manhole cover where we could climb down unseen. After about 1,500 feet we found a small manhole along the pathway. We removed our packs and I took out my crowbar. Up came the lid and we placed it off to the side. Peeking down into the hole, we could see water running about 12 feet below. It was the perfect location. The system of tunnels down there was a so-called storm drainage system, built to store water to prevent flooding during heavy downfall, but also intended to collect wastes such as oil, gas, manure, and industrial contaminates. We replaced the lid again and began our preparations. The temperature underground was warmer than on the surface, so we packed up some of our clothes. When we were all ready I extracted my crowbar once again, lifted the lid, and maneuvered it away. We climbed down and pulled the lid shut. We left a red thread hanging down as a marker in case we weren't able to find another exit.

The interlude did us good. It'd been a long time since I had relaxed so deeply. I was in such a good mood that I even thought a cigarette sounded like a good idea. I bummed one off Steve, lighted up, and inhaled. It tasted good.

As soon as we'd shut the manhole cover, the sounds of wind and rain from the park ceased and a quiet trickle was the only thing we could hear. We began walking west beneath the park. The tunnel was high enough that we could walk upright, but narrow enough that it felt most natural to walk in single file. We hadn't pulled on our waders yet, figuring that there wouldn't be too much water, but we'd underestimated the water's depth. Each of us tried scuttling along the edge of the stream, but it sloped down and we would slide into the water and get wet. The tunnel was constructed from concrete. After a while we arrived at an extensive tunnel system with large sections branching off in various directions. Some were for water, others for sewage. The barrier between the sewage and water troughs was low and the fluids spilled into each other. When it floods, it all gets mixed together down there. But this wasn't drinking water, so no harm was done.

We continued along under a street that Steve thought must be Underhill Avenue, where we'd parked the car. After two hours, we decided to take a break. I nestled in near a small waterfall. Or maybe not a waterfall, but a tunnel that was at a higher level than the one in which we had been walking and which had been built to spill into ours. The sound of the water was pleasantly hypnotizing. I was tired, so I squinted and nodded off for a while, but woke again after about five minutes and looked around. Steve had lit a cigarette and murmured quietly, almost to himself, 'When you're not worried about getting caught or dying, it's really nice being underground.' Alan and Liz were leaning back where they sat; they seemed almost dreamy. The interlude did us good. It'd been a long time since I had relaxed so deeply. I was in such a good mood that I even thought a cigarette sounded like a good idea. I bummed one off Steve, lighted up, and inhaled. It tasted good.

In an episode of the television series *The Twilight Zone*, a man builds an airtight bunker to keep out everything he considers dangerous. He moves into the bunker, locks the door, and realizes to his surprise that what scares him is no longer outside but inside the bunker. He should have come along with us under Kissena Park, stretched out, and found his peace here.

I once asked Liz what she saw in life as an urban explorer. 'For me, it's like walking along a stream in the forest. The sound and tones of the water spilling over stones, dropping from differing heights, is just like it would be if you were up on a mountain somewhere. And that's what I love about it. It's like a kind of amazing sensory deprivation experience, and afterwards you can feel your senses waking up to all kinds of small nuances and details.'

Beneath Kissena Park. Nothing in the underground has been created for the purpose of being beautiful, yet the man-made landscape has its own beauty as well.

I could empathize with her delight over small details and how easy it is to overlook them. Just like Steve, she is also fascinated by the history behind what she sees. For her, the underground is, 'a manifestation of that history. And since it's carved out of rock, it's easy to switch between thoughts of human history to natural history. The differentiation between the two starts to become unclear, which I like.'

When I returned home from the South Pole, I started to realize, without ever having thought about it, that I was practicing mindfulness, the doctrine of conscious awareness or something similar to it, both on my expeditions and even sometimes at home. I had never heard of it before, but a coincidental meeting was a turning point. Robert Pirsig, the author of *Zen and the Art of Motorcycle Maintenance*, once sat at a table next to mine in a restaurant. We began talking and he asked about my wilderness experiences. I told him about my expeditions that had taken me farther and farther away from my starting point. We exchanged books, and although his book is about the care and maintenance of motorcycles, the experience of presence in one's task is the same: 'When one isn't dominated by feelings of separateness from what he's working on, then one can be said to "care" about what he's doing. That is what caring really is, a feeling of identification with what one's doing. When one has this feeling then he also sees the inverse side of caring, Quality itself.'

As I lay stretched out near the artificial waterfall with eyes shut, listening to the timbre of flowing water, that same feeling arose again.

We continued on. I fell and became more soaked. I could see that Steve was wet, too, and that there was nowhere else to hang our clothes to dry than on our bodies. The question was whether we should try to find another exit than the one we had entered. It was possible, but we were walking below a busy street, so we finally decided to return to our starting point.

The tunnels all looked alike, with grey cement everywhere. We had a GPS device, but it only worked when we stuck the antenna up out of a manhole cover, which was a bit of a hassle. We decided to go with our gut feeling to choose the direction. I can usually trust my internal sense of direction, but not this time. The dark, murky tunnels, all seemingly identical, made me uncertain, and I was relieved when we could see the red wool thread hanging down from our manhole cover. We climbed up the ladder and came out of the tunnel. Replacing the cover, we made our way to the car. We were all drenched. My pants stuck to my legs in a temperature just above freezing. We weren't exactly swimming in opportunities to stop and dry off. I was freezing and knew that we wouldn't really warm up again until we were in the sewers at Canal Street.

Back inside the car, Alan had grown pensive. He said he found it strange that in his twenty years in New York, he'd only looked at the city from its height and breadth, but never from its third dimension, the underground. Liz and Steve discussed the best way to navigate quickly back to Midtown. Liz suggested we go via Utopia Parkway. What a great name! What dreams were that name based on?

11. CANAL STREET, MANHATTAN: SHIT!

Driving down to SoHo late Thursday evening, I texted a good friend of mine who lived in the area to ask if we could store some of our things in her apartment while we did a bit of reconnaissance for manholes around Canal Street. 'Erling, I am a Somalian woman with a Norwegian passport in New York, and I don't want to be a part of your expedition,' was the response. I could understand her sentiment, and I felt bad for trying to involve her.

For the time being, we would have to keep lugging around our equipment. The two crowbars that I'd tied to the back of my pack clanked and rattled against each other as we walked from Midtown through SoHo, high-end boutiques and loft apartments on either side of us. We'd soon be trudging through the excrement of those who lived here. I stopped, took off my backpack, and tightened the straps. My sleeping bag was packed away, safe and dry, but it would be a long time until I rolled it out again. Navigating the sewers through SoHo and Canal Street was going to take all night.

First Attempt

As its name suggests, Canal Street was originally a canal in Manhattan, but with the increasing demand for land, it was rerouted below ground. The tunnel was constructed in the early 1800s. Steve was especially keen on exploring this sewage system, as it is Manhattan's oldest.

Tonight was finally the night for the SoHo sewers around Canal Street. There was no doubt that Steve viewed this leg of the journey as our high point, beneath the small boutiques that had now closed for the evening, under the click of expensive heels on their way to restaurants. He had tried once before to get in, but had only managed a few meters before he was met by a powerful blast of warm steam and stench and a high water level. 'It is a crazy adventure just to get in,' he explained excitedly.

Steve and I discussed starting off in Greene Street, opening a manhole there and heading toward Canal Street. A good plan. As soon as we reached Canal Street, we would take a right and continue west toward Hudson River and Canal Park. Liz went home to Brooklyn. Alan had agreed to stand guard at the manhole where we planned to enter, and later at the pipe where we would climb out. He had been a journalist when he'd started on Monday, but by now he was also a part of the expedition.

There is one reason that Steve and I had never yet met with accidents or been caught by the authorities: we were careful. With just a couple of exceptions. Like the time that Moses and Steve climbed to the top of Notre Dame—with a Frenchman named Nico they met in a bar—and decided to ring the church bells. The temptation of those bells just dangling there had been too big to withstand. Steve explained to me the basic differences between French and American police: the French can empathize with the human urge to climb. In their interrogation after they had descended from the church tower, the police had been respectful and had released them in the morning. The day before our expedition, I had informed Steve about my promise to my family not to take any unnecessary risks. We hadn't known each other so well yet, and I think he was relieved to learn that I had some good common sense.

Entering and exiting the sewers in SoHo is a challenge. We could have just taken a risk, of course, opened one up, and popped down. And maybe it would have worked out. But it wasn't really our style to undertake something that might harm someone other than ourselves. So we first set about finding a location where we could suitably exit the sewer. Earlier, on our way through Canal Park to Williamsburg Bridge, we had, as mentioned, checked that the cover was loose. Alan, Steve, and I returned again after walking around Greene Street to look for loose manhole covers for our entrance.

The park was closed. It was around midnight and the area was teeming with people and traffic. We would undoubtedly be spotted if we attempted to scale the fence now. We stood waiting for a pause between passers-by, but the pause never came and Alan and I took a stroll around the block, pretending we weren't up to anything. Steve went in the opposite direction, but when we returned to the park and our manhole cover ten minutes later, we noticed a car from a private security company nearby. The car was parked with its motor running, the chauffeur sitting inside. We waited. The car didn't move. It was hard to know if they were on the lookout for us or for something else.

A stream of pedestrians and cars passed, among them several police cars. I am constantly amazed at how many policemen there are in the city. At times it can even seem like there is one policeman per inhabitant. The security car continued idling in place. We decided to give up for an hour. Alan knew of a bar some blocks away: Nancy Whiskey Pub in TriBeCa. We walked there.

Nancy Whiskey Pub looks like any other bar. The shelves behind the bar were crowded with various bottled liquors, and a cute girl mixed drinks, opened beer bottles, and served customers, a shuffleboard lined the wall and five televisions transmitted different sports shows, weather forecasts, and news briefs interspersed with commercials: *Melrose Credit Rating. Makes life easy.* The music was loud. The Botoxed cheeks of Vladimir Putin appeared on screen but I couldn't make out what he was saying. Alan ordered three Jack Daniel's, which we promptly kicked back. Steve asked for another round. I had to take a leak. Above the bathroom door was a black American flag framed by Christmas lights, and when I returned, I noticed a framed newspaper article with photos of an astronaut behind the bar. I've always been captivated by those pioneers of space in their tinny rocket ships. 'A loving husband, and devoted father,' was astronaut Mike Mullane's reply when a NASA psychologist inquired what he would like to have written on his gravestone. But deep inside, he wrote in his book *Riding Rockets*, 'I would have sold my wife and children into slavery for a ride into space.' The one doesn't necessarily exclude the other. I imagine he was probably being honest in both cases.

Alan looked disheveled where he sat, and Steve and I both looked like we resided in the underground. Our garments were coated in a coarse layer of sludge. I asked Steve his opinion: did all of the shit we had waded through conceal the city's reality, or was it the actual reality? He thought it must be the latter. I ordered three more glasses. Estelle's 'American Boy' was playing full-blast: 'Take me to Broadway/Let's go shopping, Baby, then we'll go to a café/Let's go on the subway/Take me to your hood.' A girl at the other end of the bar had been following us with her eyes as we came in, our clothes and backpacks filthy. We had hidden the crowbars from sight so as not to draw undue attention. She came over to us now to get the scoop.

'Where are you guys coming from?' she asked. 'The sewers,' said Steve, and she said, 'Yeah, right!' Steve showed her some photos from his camera. The girl shook her head in disbelief and said, 'Now... what's the point in that?' None of us replied. She asked again. 'I think it's cool,' said Steve. She stood and chatted with us. I liked Steve's answer. It reminds me of George Mallory's answer about why he wanted to climb Everest: 'Because it's there.'

Steve and me at Nancy Whiskey Pub in TriBeCa.

Christmas decor and an abundant selection of liquor behind the bar.

The bricks remain firmly packed, two hundred years after the tunnel was built.

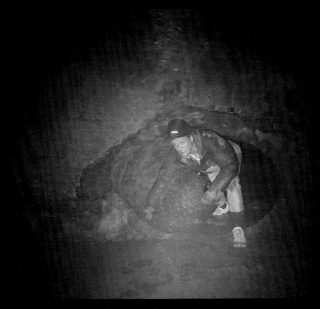

Tight quarters in the sewer below Greene Street. We come out into a larger tunnel beneath Canal Street.

Second Attempt: The Early Hours of December 17th

It was 2.30 a.m. by the time we left the bar and headed back toward Canal Park. It was quiet out and there weren't many people. No policemen or security cars. I was relieved to be able to get on with our expedition. Steve hopped the fence, uncovered the manhole that would be our exit, then returned to us. We wanted a downstream exit so we could enter the tunnels in SoHo and walk underground following the flow of the sewage. Above ground, we sauntered toward SoHo, crossing Greene Street and Grand Street back toward our manhole entrance.

An hour later, at 3.30 a.m., Steve and I disappeared below Greene and began our stooped walk toward Canal until the roof got so low we had to crawl. It eventually became even smaller, and we were forced to lie on our stomachs to wiggle further through the sewage pipe toward Canal Street. Alan remained above ground as our lookout. We had been travelling since Monday, but now it was the first time I asked myself: what am I doing here? My thoughts lingered for a few seconds, but the sewer isn't a very good place to lie around philosophizing, so I lifted my chin and looked up ahead.

We wriggled onward. Past *Rattus norvegicus*, who stood and unblinkingly looked me in the eye for a moment before darting off to find more food. Humans are the only species who have replaced the constant hunt for new food with time set aside to research and learn. Our discovery continued down through the narrow tunnel beneath Greene in the direction of Canal Street, waste smeared over our bodies. The situation was absurd: we found ourselves in a small pipe, voluntarily slithering through excrement from SoHo. But this was not the right place for a reflective pause, and I concentrated on squirming forward. Maybe it was because my face was right next to the sewage, but it seemed as if people in this part of town used a lot more toilet paper than those up in the Bronx.

A few paces ahead, I could see that the pipe widened. I squeezed through to where the ceiling yawned open to three feet in height. I continued walking, crouched over. It was hard, but not extreme. It felt like there wasn't much oxygen in the air, and I was out of breath. Although the distances weren't very far, it seemed liked time ran on another track in the sewers. Time didn't matter. It's a feeling that I only get when I'm on an expedition, and also when I am enjoying time spent with someone I love. In those situations, time seems to go neither fast nor slow. Soon, I could make out that a larger tunnel crossed ours up ahead. Steve whooped behind me. He had seen it too.

We stood in the tunnel directly under Canal Street. It felt wonderful to stand upright again. We beamed our lights around us. The tunnel was beautiful: bricks painstakingly laid in a circle all the way around. Nice handiwork, almost like the tunnel in the Bronx. A colony of cockroaches was busy on the walls, and here and there a rat scampered by. The cockroaches looked like many that I have seen all over the world, and I guessed it was the ordinary *Blatta orientalis*. Cockroaches like to move in a herd and are able to survive longer than rats. The authorities can conquer the rats by sending supersonic sounds through the tunnels. The rats are highly sensitive to sound; they go crazy with the noise and ram themselves into the walls. But cockroaches have been around since the dinosaurs and managed to survive the meteor that wiped the dinosaurs out. They are resolute, unshakeable. I have heard somewhere that there are more rats in New York than there are people, but I can't really believe it. Rats are easily exterminated. *Blatta orientalis*, on the other hand, will probably outlive us all.

Up to now, we hadn't come across any rats outside of the subway stations. But I could see that this was a good place for rats to thrive. The sewer runs so slowly that there's little danger in walking along the flow. There's also more than enough food. We directed our lights toward the rats and they darted off westward, in the direction of the sewer stream toward Canal Park.

We now had space on all sides and it seemed like it might be smooth sailing ahead. We could hear the constant motion of traffic at full speed above on Canal Street. The larger the automobile, the higher the din when the wheels met with manhole covers. At times, we could hear the distant sounds of subway trains in nearby tunnels. Farther on in the tunnel we met with other noises. We didn't know where they came from, but it seemed like there must be some logical cause. They just came and went.

There are so many noises in New York that I almost just stopped noticing them. On my way to the South Pole, the silence was so all-encompassing that I could feel and hear it. The silence I experienced there was louder than all of the noises here put together, but of more importance now was the similarity between a polar expedition and one underground beneath SoHo: they are both about finding peace, about becoming a part of one's surroundings and being present in the moment. If one can't find this peace, it's easy to lose courage or to feel claustrophobic. At this moment, being where we were almost felt natural.

Steve and I began to make our way slowly along with the sewage. In New York, almost all of the water and sewage runs with gravity and not with pumps. Just ahead of us, the pipe had been lowered, most likely because of an intersecting road built across the upper half of the pipe. We had to stoop again for some feet before it went up again. We kept on. Slowly but surely, the conditions changed around us. The steady stream of sewage abated and came more and more to a standstill. The roof seemed to slope down, lower and lower. The stench of sewage became more powerful. Whereas previously everything had blended into a single muck—excrement, toilet paper, dishwater, and anything else belonging in a sewage pipe—now things started gradually changing so that water ran swiftly on top and the filth and solid bits clumped together underneath, forming a thick, muddy sludge. It was like slogging through a marsh. Further up ahead, the roof depressed even more and walking once again became difficult. In addition to the layer of water, the sewage now included more

---

When Dante opened his eyes, he could see souls fleeing. When we looked, we saw stagnant trash and wobbling, empty bottles, no souls fleeing. Even the rats steered clear of this muck. Rats are clean creatures, actually.

---

trash. Aside from the stationary sea of bobbing empty bottles, it wasn't easy to identify other items of trash.

We navigated the new mass but it had become strenuous to move. We were bowed over in the tunnel while trying to lift our legs out of the suction of the muddy sewage. It smelled like confined trash and feces. The combination of everything—the intrusive odor, the low ceiling, the almost impermeable sewage, all of the trash bobbing about but not going anywhere, the silence that was broken by a rumble of wheels overhead or from somewhere far off—suddenly made me laugh. Steve smiled. We wondered aloud about the length of this stagnant quagmire but neither of us had any real idea. We illuminated the tunnel ahead of us. A thick layer of fog hovered in the air, created from the warmth of the sewage and the chill air. We could only see ahead by six or seven feet.

Dante and Virgil looked at something similar after travelling for a long way down through hell. "'And now," he said, "stretch straight/your strings of sight across this age-old scum/To where the fumes are thickest, stinging most.'" When Dante opened his eyes, he could see souls fleeing. When we looked, we saw stagnant trash and wobbling, empty bottles, no souls fleeing. Even the rats steered clear of this muck. Rats are clean creatures, actually.

For the first time it dawned on me that this might be dangerous. I checked our air gauge. It didn't indicate any danger, but I don't know much about poisonous gases, and I asked myself whether it was wise to continue further. I posed the question to Steve. I assumed that poisonous gases and a lack of oxygen would increase where sewage was gathered motionless, where there was little airflow and a lack of space between the sewage and the roof of the pipe. There was especially a danger of hydrogen sulfide (H_2S), which is also called swamp gas, since the gas develops in still water. Inhaling too much of the gas can have deadly consequences.

We stood looking in through the fog. I didn't relish the thought of creeping through the cramped space and then having my alarm sound. If that happened, we would be hard-pressed to get to safety quickly. Or was I being a wimp—or too lazy? I remembered my promise to Ingrid, Solveig, and Nor about being careful. This was just the type of situation that my promise had entailed. I explained my thoughts to my companion. We discussed it back and forth and decided to err on the side of caution.

Steve snapped a few photos while I held our equipment. After a while, I padded over to a manhole tunnel and stood upright up to the top. Steve followed, and we attempted to call Alan, who was holding watch up in Greene Street. But Alan didn't answer his phone. We began to backtrack. A few minutes later, we reached him. Something had gone wrong with his phone, so we told him that we had turned around and asked him to keep watch so we wouldn't be hit by any cars when we tried climbing up again.

Walking in the opposite direction under Canal Street was better, now that we knew what to expect. We soon arrived back where the sewer ran from under Greene Street. The same cockroaches clung to the walls. They looked the same, anyway. Cockroaches check in, they don't check out. We took a break and tried to take some photos, but the damp air steamed up the lens.

I stooped over and began making my way up the tunnel beneath Greene. Steve had suggested to Alan that we try exiting through a manhole closer to Canal so we wouldn't have to go all the way back. In Canal Street, there was so much traffic that an attempt to come out there might risk a car wheel to the head. We found a manhole toward the end of Greene. We both crowded into the upward-leading tunnel and stood upright, packed closely against each other. I looked into Steve's eyes, they seemed bluer than usual in his filth-covered face. We asked ourselves whether the manhole here was far enough away from Canal Street for a safe exit. After a bit of discussion, we agreed that this was wishful thinking, so I bowed out, back into the low tunnel, and continued navigating forward. We would soon reach the very small part of the tunnel. I walked in a squat for a few paces before I finally lay down on my stomach and pulled myself along the base. It was easier this time. We were already used to the wiggling motion now. We inched forward. Steve was a few feet behind me. Suddenly, I saw a white iPhone. Not only do they use more toilet paper in SoHo than in the Bronx, they also throw their iPhones down the toilet. I left it there. A bit further I also saw a gun cartridge just below my chin. What is the story behind that, I wondered, from the time it was bought in the gun shop until it ended up under my nose here in SoHo. I left it there too. I was busy enough making my way forward. I tried to lie as low on my chest as possible to avoid scraping the top of the tunnel, where excrement and muck hung in globs. But the tunnel was too low and I couldn't avoid it. At the same time, I had to hold my head high enough to keep my chin from shoveling through the sewage.

As I squirmed, I heard the faint noises from a nearby manhole a bit farther ahead getting louder. I came to the manhole tunnel and stood up. Steve arrived soon after and stood beside me. A manhole is meant for one person, and it was tight with two. We stood squeezed in, sewage trickling down our ankles, our torsos stuck to each other in the narrow passageway up to the manhole cover. Neither of us said anything or moved; we were listening for cars. If we heard too many cars passing, we would have to find another manhole to exit. Minutes passed, and after a while Steve thought we should risk it.

He took out a little red flag tied to a metal stick. It was home-made and intended for occasions such as this. He shoved the flag up through a hole in the cover. We could hear voices above us. We were unsure what it was and decided to sit tight for a few more minutes. The voices were talking to each other. Then we heard Alan's voice: 'Everything's clear!' I climbed up and tried to push the cover aside, but it was stuck. I systematically pounded against the edges of the cover, pressed again and again with my shoulder. It wouldn't budge. I twirled around one hundred and eighty degrees so I was upside down and pressed out with my feet. But it was still stuck. Steve took over and continued pounding on the cover. It finally gave way. I could tell that Steve's shoulder was hurting after that little battle with the manhole cover. He climbed up and I followed, but stopped when I was halfway out. Steve wanted to film. I waited in the manhole opening while he set up his equipment.

Alan had found an orange plastic traffic cone and placed it up ahead of the traffic so that drivers could think we were doing some construction work and slow down. Steve filmed. I climbed out, replaced the manhole cover, took the traffic cone, and walked briskly over to the sidewalk. Steve wanted to do another take, so he could take photos too. I was skeptical and refused. Alan, Steve, and I had just managed to sit down on a metal staircase leading from the sidewalk up to some office buildings when a police car rounded the corner onto the cobblestones of Greene Street.

We sat back and followed the car with our eyes. The cover was in place, the street looked the same as always, and the police car continued driving without stopping. If we'd been seen exiting the manhole, we would have been arrested immediately and taken before a judge to explain ourselves. I breathed a sigh of relief. Trespassing through sewers is hardly a serious misdemeanor, but it would have been unpleasant anyway. I looked around. There were sprinklers on the windows behind us. Two security cameras filmed the scene, if they weren't just there for show—they looked real. Across the street was a parking spot, and just in front of it, a lone tree had managed to press itself into the façade of a worn-down house. How exactly had this tree managed to survive? How did it come to grow in this spot? What was the source of its nourishment? For me, the tree was a quiet symbol of the New York we had seen: '[...] life under difficulties, growth against odds, sap-rise in the midst of concrete, and the steady reaching for the sun,' as E. B. White wrote in the essay *Here is New York*.

A post office sat on the opposite side of Canal Street. The building had a touch of imperial Roman style, with high columns that seemed liberated from the rest of the building's architecture. It seems to me that a lot of Americans enjoy references to this epoch. Maybe the Greco-Roman columns that Americans put on post offices, universities, libraries, and houses serve to bring a feeling of tradition and safety? Just like the wild-west aesthetic of the fire and police stations near Williamsburg Bridge, which call to mind a time when the new continent was conquered. I think there might be something to this theory.

A Black Cat Crosses the Path

I felt relieved and happy. Was it possible that I was about to end the happiest day or night of my life? Without even realizing it? 'In fact no one recognizes the happiest moment of their lives as they are living it. It may well be that, in a moment of joy, one might sincerely believe that they are living that golden instant "now", even having lived such a moment before, but whatever they say, in one part of their hearts they still believe in the certainty of a happier moment to come,' writes the Turkish Nobel laureate, Orhan Pamuk, in the book *The Museum of Innocence*. I agree. The first sentence in the book is: 'It was the happiest moment of my life, though I didn't know it.' The author dwells on the difficulty of living, especially if one is young and believes that everything might only get worse. Late in his life, Kemal, the main character, realizes that the happiest moment in his life was when he was thirty and went to bed with a distant relative that he fell helplessly in love with just before his own wedding. He was supposed to help her with her schoolwork, but things turned out differently.

Kemal remains in love with the woman. They don't end up together, but he nonetheless spends 1,593 evenings (yes, you read it correctly) in her company, together with her parents, and usually her husband as well, in their home. I despaired a bit on his behalf as I read the book. As he summarizes these evenings, he writes: 'I remember each and every evening I went to supper—even the most difficult, most hopeless, most humiliating evenings—as happiness.'

I stood up from the metal stairway, lifted the straps that held my waders in place on my shoulders, and tried pulling the pants carefully down over my body, around my legs and feet so as to avoid the most filthy parts. It was impossible. The back of my jacket and my hat were both caked in excrement. There was simply poop everywhere.

There's nowhere on SoHo's streets to wash or rinse yourself or your clothes. I decided to throw away my gloves, which were sopping wet. I had brought along a pair of mittens in case it was extra-cold. Steve looked on amazed and shook his head. He asked if he could have my gloves. Of course he was right; all I had to do was wash them out after the trip and they would be good as new. I regretted my decision, but finders are keepers, and I didn't say anything more about it. We folded our waders together and put them into our plastic bags. I slapped my hat against the stairs to scrape off the worst of the muck before putting it in my bag. After some slaps, I had successfully displaced sewage from the underground via my hat to the stairway where we were sitting. A large black cat crossed our path on the other side of the street as we walked past the parking spot toward Canal Street. If I had been superstitious, I might have taken this as an ill omen, but as a friend of mine puts it: 'A cat is black on one day, grey the next, and maybe white on the third.' So I didn't let it worry me.

We hadn't planned on showering for the length of the journey, so it was pointless to think too much about how odd it was to stand sporting sewage in SoHo. There was nothing for it but to continue on. Our underground excursion had taken a long time; it was now 5.30 a.m. We decided to go get Jackie, who wanted to join us in the next leg of our trip. Signaling a taxi, we placed our bags in the trunk. The driver didn't seem to mind the clank of our crowbars and we directed him to take us to Brooklyn, where Jacki lives.

The tunnel under Canal Street gets progressively smaller, the air becomes more dense, and the sewage rises as we get close to the Hudson River.

Snapshot of my hat, soaked with shit.

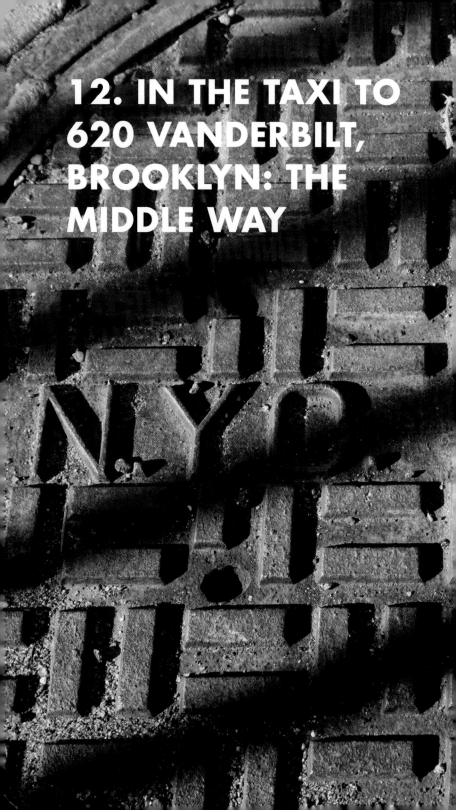

12. IN THE TAXI TO 620 VANDERBILT, BROOKLYN: THE MIDDLE WAY

Those of us who are modern Westerners—people like you, Steve, and me—often go around harboring two opposing impulses at once. We wish, on the one hand, to tear ourselves away from our community, and on the other we want to be a part of it. We want to free ourselves from others' expectations of us, to take control of the situations in our lives rather than be controlled by them. We want to feel as though we are unique, to live without being bored, and we would like to privatize our own moral constraints in the way that Steve and I did as we, without qualms, snuck in and out of the sewers below the sleeping population of SoHo. To decide for oneself, for the most part, what is right and wrong.

'I see myself as a kind of Robin Hood,' said Steve in his smooth voice while on the taxi ride. 'I like to discover places that are rich in history and to share them with people who often seem to lack connections with the past. When I first started out, it was all about excitement, but now it's about the history of places and telling the story about them that is most important for me. I know that I am doing something unlawful, but I feel like I am doing something good. The truly criminal thing is not to see the amazing world that is below.'

We want to be our own masters, but we also want to justify our lives, to be seen and to partake as members of society, to receive applause and recognition. For this, we gladly relinquish portions of our personal freedom. We do it when we decide to have families, for instance, when we arrive at work at the same time each morning, go work out together, and lie down to sleep at home. Freedom and the desire to belong may seem like opposites, but they are also connected.

Could it be that there is a middle way, a solution like the one that Aristotle wrote about as the right path between our urge for freedom and our need for belonging? Ziyad Marar, the author of *The Happiness Paradox*, poses this question, too, and his answer is no. We left that opportunity behind us long ago. Therefore, he maintains, we humans will always be pulled back and forth between our opposing natures, never quite satisfied. Marar claims that the tension between these two desires is much greater today than at any other point in history. But I think he exaggerates the differences between ancient times and today. Every generation makes claims that former times used to be easier, but I think that the task of finding a middle way has always had its challenges.

Finding the Middle Way Ain't Easy

As far as I've read, Aristotle never wrote about any golden mean, but there are nonetheless a lot of people who refer to his golden mean. In any case, the idea makes sense. However, neither you

---

Skiing to the poles, sailing the Atlantic and down to Antarctica, or scaling Mount Everest became, after a while, a humdrum task. Frost, hunger, uncertainty, and toil. The days were the same and eventually blended into one another.

---

nor I can decide where the middle way is supposed to be. According to Aristotle, this is only for wise men to decide. Nowadays, I am not sure who these wise men are. And meanwhile the challenge still remains, that it is often difficult to know where the middle way lies. Is it to be found walking to the North Pole, working long shifts at your job, or starting a family? What is the right amount of goodwill to have? At the foundation of Aristotle's thinking is the premise that the advantages and disadvantages of any choice should be divisible and definable. Having done this, you and I should then be able to choose a middle way between them. But when you're lying in sewage below Greene Street, the matter of deciphering positives and negatives isn't always crystal-clear, and reaching a choice isn't so simple. The situation is dark and cramped and murky, and everything kind of blends together. Sometimes it seems like Aristotle ignored the value of making bad decisions. He was only interested in the correct choices,

---

I have often been most happy when I've chosen some extreme alternative, swearing off the middle way and taking a decision that many might consider dumb.

---

but bad decisions are also an important part of life. Having 'bad' friends and shitting in the face of society's expectations also has its own kind of value. I had no doubts as I sat there in the back of the taxi. Maybe I should try to learn more from these experiences. They have undoubtedly provided me with both joys and sorrows throughout my life, but without the negative experiences I would have missed out on some of the good things.

I have often been most happy when I've chosen some extreme alternative, swearing off the middle way and taking a decision that many might consider dumb: here in New York, for example, or out sailing across oceans, or climbing mountains. It's the same in everyday life. One extreme example from daily life was becoming a father. It's also the only experience that can occur over and over again and still be just as great every time.

On the other hand, constantly pushing boundaries can even become routine and lose its thrill over time. This is something I noticed after I'd gone on expeditions for several years. Skiing to the poles, sailing the Atlantic and down to Antarctica, or scaling Mount Everest became, after a while, a humdrum task. Frost, hunger, uncertainty, and toil. The days were the same and eventually blended into one another. Even polar explorers, mountain climbers, and extreme-sport enthusiasts can benefit from finding balance—a middle way between being at home and being in nature—to find meaning in life.

13. QUEENS STORM DRAIN, QUEENS: THE PAST LIVES ON

We woke Jacki. She opened her window to see who was knocking. Her hair was matted and she looked exhausted, but she took it in good stride and served us some coffee. It might have been the first time that Steve had been on time. I washed my hands thoroughly. Used a lot of soap and scrubbed my fingers. My hands had been scratched in several places over the past days and I wanted to steer clear of infection. When I finished, my hands were sparkling clean but her sink looked like it had aged a few years. Steve went in to the bathroom for his turn at the sink. We were all hungry, and crossed the street for fried eggs and more coffee. Andrew and Brent joined us after a while at the diner. We all jumped into Andrew's car, two up front and four squeezed in back, with our backpacks and gear in a huddle. We drove east to the Queens Storm Drain at Brookville Park. The plan was to locate a manhole there and to walk out toward the Atlantic Ocean following the stream of shit, tampons, empty bottles, and toilet paper we'd waded through en route. All of the water we'd walked through ultimately flows out to the Atlantic Ocean, and we planned to follow it to the end of its route.

Up until this point, we had mostly navigated without any underground maps, but this time we had a map of the water tunnels. It was hard to figure it out, though, and it seemed like the area might have changed since the map had been drawn up. I don't know how old it was, or where it came from, but it didn't seem very useful. We drove up and down the streets, trying to locate the right manhole. We were only a few miles from John F. Kennedy International Airport and we didn't want to attract attention, especially since we didn't especially look like people from the neighborhood or who were planning to hop on a flight. According to its website, Homeland Security is tasked with 'securing the nation from the many threats we face,' and to that end is responsible with securing the safety in areas surrounding American airports. We weren't eager to encounter any of that gang, so we waited until we found a remote parking spot under a grove of trees and got out. Andrew locked the car and we entered the grove to go manhole-hunting. According to the location of manholes we had spotted, the tunnel was supposed to lead to where we now stood. We were happy to find a cover, but were quickly disappointed to see that it stopped short and led to nowhere. There was only a small space beneath the cover, but no tunnel. I had become so accustomed to the manholes as a way into an alternative world that I was almost shocked at finding a barrier here.

I kept a lookout for manholes that we could climb up quickly if the situation became dangerous. When I looked over at Steve and Andrew, I could tell they were doing the same.

We split up to continue our search and soon discovered a hole that would work. We could hear water running below when we pried it open. Andrew, Brent, Steve, and I lowered ourselves down. The cover was put back in place. It was a modern cement tunnel. We walked a ways inland and took a look around before turning and heading in the other direction, out toward Jamaica Bay and a small piece of the Atlantic. After barely an hour, Brent had collected all the sound he needed and went back to climb out of the tunnel where we'd entered. The three of us continued.

The tide that pushed inward toward us increased in speed and the water level rose gradually. Andrew and I had waders on, but Steve didn't. The water was cold now in the wintertime. Steve was drenched and freezing. He walked and chastised himself for not bringing his waders, too. We weren't sure how much farther it was, but we soon realized that the tidal waters might get so powerful as to be dangerous. I looked up at the brick wall overhead and saw the line indicating how high the water could reach at high tide. It would be difficult to breathe well, swimming in such high water below the ceiling, and I was reminded that the tunnels aren't made with human explorers in mind. We picked up the pace. It was heavy going. Andrew complained about one of his shoes that had gotten stuck somewhere and disappeared. But we kept going. Trying to find the shoe again would have been futile. I kept a lookout for manholes that we could climb up quickly if the situation became dangerous. When I looked over at Steve and Andrew, I could tell they were doing the same.

We Came from the Past

I thought I could see light up ahead. All of us thought it must be daylight. After a while, we saw several parallel water tunnels converging ahead, with sunlight streaming though the columns that separated them from one another. From far away, the lighted-up columns looked fantastical. They were bathed in golden light while everything else around us was dark. It felt as though they belonged in another realm, and in the low afternoon light they almost resembled ruins. As we got closer, we saw what we'd already suspected, that they were merely functional columns made of cement. We continued as best we could and we soon arrived. On our left was the sea and to the right, blue sky at the end of the tunnel.

Steve and I hugged each other. Then we gave Andrew a hug. Some ways away, we could hear the sound of a powerful airplane motor. We glanced up. An American Airlines plane, with its characteristic aluminum color, pulled in for a landing directly above our heads. We became uncertain. How close to the airport were we, exactly? The three of us clambered up the slope from the water, where we discovered that we were only six or seven feet away. A single black security fence separated us from the airport. Steve, Andrew, and I exchanged glances, none of us doubting what needed to happen next: we had to get out of there.

We had to climb over the back fence and get out before Homeland Security noticed us.

But the situation was even more serious than we'd thought. Not only were we facing a security fence, but there was one behind us as well. We had surfaced between both fences in an area that was supposed to keep out unwanted guests. Looking over at the others, it wasn't hard to discern their thoughts: we had to climb over the back fence and get out before Homeland Security noticed us. Fortunately, fence number two looked a bit shabbier than the first one. We looked for weaknesses in the fence as we ran toward it. My heart pounded in my chest, harder than usual. Up above a gate we could see that the barbed wire was slightly separated. We heaved our backpacks across, pulled on our gloves to protect our hands, and threw ourselves quickly over the gate. Down on the other side, we gathered our breath for a few seconds before sprinting across the street that ran parallel to the fence and running into the forest. We were finally able to relax a bit and walked slowly back to the car.

Back at the car, we met Alan, Jacki, and Brent. Everyone smiled widely and I gave each of them a hug. The expedition was over, and it had been a success. 'Good adventuring! Next time, you guys should go somewhere crazy—like the past,' said Andrew, standing there in one shoe. 'No,' I said. 'We just came from the past. The past lives on, down in the underground.' I stood and remembered the most beautiful set of sentences I've ever read, the last words in the novel *The Great Gatsby*:

'... *tomorrow we will run faster, stretch out our arms farther...*
And one fine morning—
So we beat on, boats against the current, borne back cease-
lessly into the past.'

The expedition is over, and Steve and I give each other a big hug. But then we decide to take an extra trip into a train tunnel in East New York.

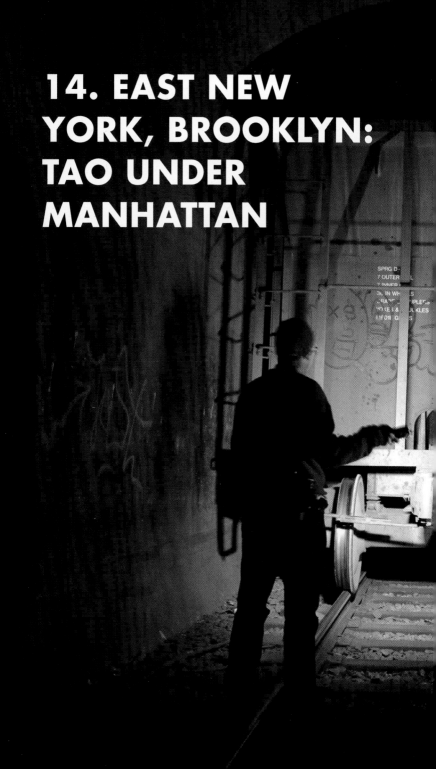

14. EAST NEW YORK, BROOKLYN: TAO UNDER MANHATTAN

It was Friday afternoon, the fifth day of our journey. We hadn't slept since we'd woken up at Brooklyn's place on Thursday morning, but I was so elated that I hardly felt tired. And we hadn't yet visited the underground in the part of town that shared her name. Steve must have been thinking the same thing, and he asked me: 'Should we continue?' Yes, I said. Sometimes it's hard to stop once you've really gotten going. I like to think of my journeys without any obvious start and end points. The least interesting part of reaching the South Pole is arriving. When I stood there at the South Pole, hanging on to my ski poles after roughly seven weeks alone, I almost felt good enough to have kept on going to the North Pole. But only almost.

We went to Moses's apartment at Lincoln Place, near Franklin Avenue in Brooklyn, and cracked open a couple of beers. He wasn't home, but we had a key. 'Should we shower?' Steve asked. 'If we do,' I said, 'then the trip is over. We won't keep going after that.' Steve agreed. We went out again.

As we walked back to Franklin Avenue, I told Steve an old story I'd read. Someone asks an old Zen master what it means to become enlightened. The master takes a stick and hits him on the head. What he wanted to teach was this: the secrets of life cannot be described; they take the form of events that happen to you. The old philosophies never offered a compiled answer of how one should live. That's in contrast to the happiness industry that is rampant today, which cashes in on describing paths to certain happiness, like street signs. Instead, the old philosophies contented themselves with thought experiments, experiences, and some techniques.

It was still light out, so there weren't many places we could go undetected. We checked out a few subway stations, but there are too many people in a large city at rush hour to simply climb over the gate without a dozen spectators. Steve suggested we hail a taxi to East New York. All the way to Brooklyn. I nodded. Trying out new ground sounded like a good idea.

In the taxi, Steve told me that East New York is one of the few areas in the city that still has a fair share of blatant crime. I couldn't have cared less. I figured that most of the bandits roaming around in Brooklyn, as in most places, had enough sense to rob people who looked like they had something to steal. I was flying high and had a bit of the same feeling I'd discovered upon my trek to the South Pole: that my path had become a part of me and I a part of it. That I was present where I was at, and could sense what was going on around me with my entire being, and that I felt safe and relaxed.

The mood in the taxi was high. The expedition had been completed. And now we were heading out on a little bonus tour.

The Last Journey

Urban planning was apparently not the highest priority in this part of town, and it was difficult to find our way. Dusk had already fallen as we began looking for subway tracks, and few people were out on the street. As far as we could tell, they were mostly Afro-Americans and people of Caribbean descent. They looked the way that poor people are often portrayed in movies: dirty, with worn-out clothes and a somewhat empty or despondent gaze. I was sure that the area had more to offer but we didn't have time to explore.

Up ahead, we found our way along the railway tracks cut off

by new barbed-wire fences. Almost six feet high, with circular barbed wire at the top. As usual. Someone internal to the barbed-wire industry must have made a fortune in this city. Fortunately, whoever had strung the wire had left a few openings for people like us. We found a tree growing close to the fence, and we climbed over by supporting ourselves against the trunk and maneuvering ourselves across the top.

It was dark out and a few people stood milling around outside a worksite 60 feet away, but they were looking in the other direction when we hopped the fence.

Several railway tracks lay parallel, but when we checked the tracks with our flashlights, we could see that they were rarely used. They were rusty and covered by a thin layer of grime. That could be a good thing. Ahead of us were several tunnels with one track each. We entered one of them. Just inside were the remains of what used to be someone's residence. Some clothes, a mattress,

---

The tunnel was quiet, and suddenly the beams of our flashlights hit upon a gigantic train that stood directly in front of us. We were both startled, although the train was parked.

---

and a bit of trash, but the place seemed to have been abandoned by its homeless owner. Anyone who could cross the fence had most likely been chased away. The graffiti painters, on the other hand, had increased their presence. We stood taking in the myriad paintings and even recognized some of the signatures from artwork in other tunnels. It looked as if REVS had been here, too. We continued on into the tunnel, and the graffiti disappeared soon after. Apparently, the graffiti painters prefer working toward the end of the tunnels. We chatted back and forth. We were both so buoyant that we felt wide awake. We had so many memories from the last days, and we laughed and discussed them. Like me, Steve was relieved that everything had gone well. We hadn't done any damage and none of the participants had had any accidents.

The tunnel was quiet, and suddenly the beams of our flashlights hit upon a gigantic train that stood directly in front of us. We were both startled, although the train was parked. Oncoming trains were something we'd both actively tried to avoid at all times. The train filled the whole tunnel, and we decided to head into a side tunnel in order to get past. After about five or six hundred feet we came out the other side and could once again see the sky. This was apparently a holding place for retired trains on tracks. Curious, we climbed around on them for a while.

In a way, the expedition was at its end, but we couldn't see any easy way to exit from the railway system. The area was fenced in. A metro route ran on one side of us, elevated a five to ten feet above ground level. We were separated from it by a stretch of barbed-wire fence, and we couldn't figure out how to cross it safely. On the other side, a small vertical rock face closed us in, and we weren't sure how to scale that, either. They had done a good job of making this area secure and almost impossible to enter or exit. We turned and looked at the tunnel we had just come out of. There was a route up along the opening. It wouldn't be difficult, and wasn't very dangerous, but a little fall could spoil the whole trip. Steve and I are both fairly good technical climbers and first scrambled up the stone wall and around the tunnel opening. The wall was uneven and it was easy to get good holds. I fastened the chest strap of my backpack to keep my balance and followed Steve. We got up, climbed farther back a ways, hopped a fallen fence, and ended up outside the gardens of a few residential houses. We walked past and came out onto a street we didn't know.

Now it was over. This was it. We agreed to look for a bar now, but most places that looked like eateries were closed and there were barely any people around. Still, we were having a good time and continued walking and talking up along what I believe must have been Bushwick Avenue, which runs parallel to Broadway. It was dark, and the residential buildings were two or three stories high, decked out with lighted-up Santa Clauses, angels, and plastic Christmas trees. The neighbors must have been competing to have the biggest, flashiest decorations for Christmas.

'And with no care for any rest, we climbed—/he first, I following—until I saw,/through a round opening, some of those things/ of beauty Heaven bears. It was from there/that we emerged, to see—once more—the stars.' Thus ends the first part of Dante's journey, as he and his companion emerge from hell. A place without stars is, for him, a place without time, and when the stars once again appear in the text, it is a sign of hope. The stars are there to help the two travelers navigate. On that night in Brooklyn, there were too many lights from the buildings, cars, and billboards to see the stars, but the Christmas lights offered a pleasing alternative.

Everything Under the Sun Is New

We criss-crossed for an hour or two until we walked past one of the places Steve lived in when he first moved to New York. The area resembled East New York, but with less trash, and many of the houses that we observed were being restored. Steve talked about his life as a young man alone in the city, and I could tell that he was moved by his own words. When he first arrived in the city, he'd had much more civilized ambitions than being an urban explorer. He had wanted to study and get an office job. But then his goals changed.

I quoted a sentence from the French Renaissance writer Michel de Montaigne's essay, 'On Experience,' which I had memorized: 'Life should be an aim unto itself, a purpose unto itself.' We both liked the way it sounded, and Steve asked me what I thought Montaigne meant by it. I didn't have a good answer, but I thought aloud as we continued walking: 'Question what you are told, break your own rules, everything under the sun is new, value what you have, have passion, don't undervalue your own opportunities, and, last but not least, read and discover! Remember that you will die, but don't be afraid of your own death, accept that the meaning of life is in the living, the world isn't what it appears to be, the world is as you are. Remember: Adam was the first big explorer. He left Paradise because he was curious and wanted to meet more girls and see the world. Take a trip through the underground in New York, begin in the sewers and don't stop until you're up to your hips in saltwater.'

Steve looked at me strangely. It sounded like our own Tao under Manhattan.

Later on, we found a restaurant in Franklin Avenue near Lincoln Place and each ordered a burger. We were thirsty and gulped down a few beers. 'Oh how pale is language and how paltry/For [...] what I saw/My words are not enough' is the end of Dante's travels in Paradise. It's easier to describe hell. An Icelandic student at the next table became interested in us. She must have been following our conversation, and asked what we'd gotten out of our trip. I don't believe in final conclusions. We are changing all the time. And our experiences also change as time goes by, so she didn't receive a good answer. The last bite had been taken and enough was enough. Liz would receive an unshowered Steve. I sauntered back to Moses's place and finished the trip just as I had begun it, lying in my sleeping bag on his much-too-short leather sofa.

15. POST-NEW YORK: LONG JOURNEYS ARE ABOUT FINDING THE WAY HOME

Upon my return to Norway, I travelled to the mountains with my three daughters, and together we went cross-country skiing on the vast mountain plateau of Hardangervidda. This was the opposite of being underground in Manhattan: here we were in a pristine, white landscape, beneath a high heaven, breathing crisp, clean air. We arrived at Finse Station just as the evening dusk stretched across the mountain. There I met Egil Kolbjørnsen, one of the two stationmasters here at Norway's highest elevated train station, and bought tickets back to Oslo. I have met him before, and have always been struck at how content he seems. I asked what his trick was: 'To be healthy and able to go to work in the morning,' he told me. But then he looked at the landscape and at my daughters, thought a bit more, and added: 'Nice surroundings, good relationships with those I love, and a short commute to work.' He lives in the station building. With that simple explanation, Egil summed up what today's experts have been discovering from their research, and what philosophers in ad 2500 will still be emphasizing as ingredients for a good life.

Standing on the platform, looking out toward the winter night, I again felt the peculiar serenity of a train station as the train draws close. I looked down at the tracks. Soon they would begin to vibrate almost imperceptibly, then gradually more, up until the moment the train rumbles, screeching, into the station. The stars cast a dark-blue, shadowless light over the mountains. Egil had found his way. I'm still getting there.

MAP OF OUR COURSE

1. Van Cortlandt Park, 242nd Street, Bronx
2. Bronx sewer
3. Harlem: Columbia University
4. Central Park
5. Lower East Side, Manhattan
6. Williamsburg Bridge
7. Westside Tunnel, Manhattan
8. Kissena Park, Queens
9. Canal Street, Manhattan
10. Queens Storm Drain, Queens
11. East New York, Brooklyn

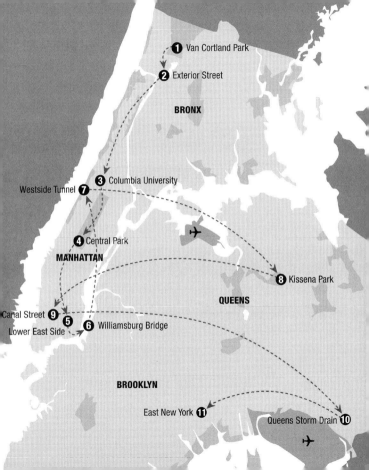

NOTES

Chapter 1. A Little Contemporary Archeology Expedition
The quote from Aristotle about living in accordance with your virtues is from *Nicomachean Ethics*, 1101a 10.
The quote from Goethe is taken from Pascal Bruckner: *Perpetual Euphoria*

Chapter 2. Van Cortlandt Park, 242nd Street, Bronx: North of the North Pole
Richard Ford wrote about the importance of doing something wrong in 'Wildlife,' *Atlantic Monthly Press*, 1990. I like Ford, but wasn't familiar with this citation until Morton A. Strøksnes told me about the article.

Chapter 3. The Bronx Sewers: Paradise Is Where I Am
Joseph Conrad's *Heart of Darkness* was originally published by William Blackwood & Sons in 1902.
Henry David Thoreau was an author, poet, and anarchist, and was concerned with civil engagement, the right to refuse to pay taxes, and non-violent protests. *Walden* is his main work, but I got the citation from a Christmas card I received from an American friend. The original quote is actually, 'The question is not what you look at, but what you see,' and is taken from Thoreau's *Journal*, August 5th, 1851.
The citation from Søren Kierkegaard's *Either/Or: A Fragment of Life* is from the translation by Alastair Hannay, Penguin Classics (1992), but the quote (and the translation) has been slightly altered, or 'Norwegianized' by me to say 'the root of all wisdom' instead of 'the sum and substance of all philosophy,' as was originally translated by Hannay.

Chapter 4. Harlem: The Philosophy Department at Columbia University

The Aristotle quotation about *eudaimonia* is from *Nicomachean Ethics*, 1098a 18.

The idea from Aristotle about the pros and cons of any choice is taken from *Ethics*, Penguin (1955), together with the introduction by Jonathan Barnes.

The quote from Ziyad Marar is from *The Happiness Paradox*, Reaktion Books (2003), p. 33

Chapter 5. Central Park: Galapagos Syndrome

The research that I refer to in the subchapter 'Achieving Happiness By Being Better Off than Your Neighbor' was from an article by Tim Harford that I read in the *Financial Times* (August 14th–15th, 2010). The study which the article refers to, concluded that many students at Harvard would rather live with poor economic standards as long as others have even less than they, than to be wealthy among other people who are better off than they are, was conducted by social economists Sara J. Solnick and David Hemenway. In a similar study by Dutch social economist Peter Kuhn and three of his colleagues, another example of the same conclusion was reached: the chance that someone will purchase a car increases if his or her neighbor has won money in the lottery in the previous six months.

Nattavudh Powdthavee, *The Happiness Equation*, quote taken from p. 137. Icon Books, 2010.

The citation of Adam Smith in the subchapter 'A Little Galapagos Syndrome' is from his *Theory of Moral Sentiments*, Empire Books (2011).

The Epicurus Reader by the Hackett Publishing Company (1994) was referenced regarding Epicurus, in particular his claim that the consequences of pleasure are often greater than the pleasure itself.

The English translation used for the quote from Franz Kafka's story 'The Departure,' originally titled '*Der Aufbruch*,' is by Tania and James Stern.

Chapter 6. Lower East Side, Manhattan: Don't Do What Your Mother Tells You

New York Magazine and *Vanity Fair* both published comprehensive profiles on Lady Gaga in 2010 (in April and September, respectively). The citations are from these articles.

Chapter 7. Williamsburg Bridge: The Use of Climbing Mount Everest

The English quote by Leo Tolstoy was taken from his *Diary*, dated February 29th, 1897. This was found at *Art as Technique* found at http://www.vahidnab.com/defam.htm. Viktor B. Sjklovski was not only a literary theorist but also a film director, author, and the founder of Russian formalism. He quotes Tolstoy in *Moderne Litteraturteori*, edited by Arild Linneberg, Arne Melberg, and Hans H. Skei, Universitetsforlaget (1991).

I haven't been able to find the original source of George Mallory's quote on the use of climbing, but his quotation is reproduced in a number of books and on the Internet, and is credited to him. I am happy each time I read it, especially since he was the first explorer I've come across who didn't insist on trying to contextualize his expedition in a larger context in order to excuse his adventurous spirit. It's hard to find explorers nowadays who don't first and foremost insist that their motivation is primarily about research, the environment, charity, children, or peace. The citation to his wife is from the book *In the Footsteps of Mallory and Irvine: The Wildest Dream: The Ghost of Everest* by Mark Mackenzie, Published by John Murray (2009).

The statement from Philippe Petit about the will to live is from his book *To Reach the Clouds*, Skyhorse Publishing (2008), reissued on the occasion of the film *Man on Wire*. The second citation is from the film.

The quote is taken from Alice Munro's story 'Too Much Happiness', published by Chatto & Windus in the collection *Too Much Happiness* in 2009.

Chapter 8. Westside Tunnel, aka Freedom Tunnel, Manhattan

Arthur Schopenhauer wrote about happiness and a lot of other stuff in his principal work *Die Welt als Wille und Vorstellung* (1819) (English translation: *The World As Will and Representation*). The excerpt from this book was published in the article 'On the Variety and Suffering of Life' in *Happiness: Classic and Contemporary Reading in Philosophy*, Oxford University Press (2007). The citation about the three biggest happinesses in life is from this article. Schopenhauer also wrote about happiness in his *Essays and Aphorisms*. This is much more fun to read than the heavy *Die Welt als Wille und Vorstellung*. The citation about ownership and the reference to how meaningless it can seem to obtain the object of one's desire is taken from here.

Chapter 9. Around 100th Street, Manhattan: Birthday with Brooklyn

This interpretation of Buddha's quotes has been done together with Egil Lothe, supervisor at the Buddhist Association (Buddhistforbundet) in Norway. He has further clarified that the word 'craving' in the quote 'To eliminate suffering, eliminate craving,' can be substituted with 'greed' or 'frustration.'

The citation from *Hamlet* by William Shakespeare is from Act II, Scene II. ('Beggar that I am, I am even poor in thanks.')

The quote by Marcus Aurelius is from *Meditations*.

Chapter 10. Kissena Park, Queens: Happiness Seems Overrated

Robert Pirsig's novel *Zen and the Art of Motorcycle Maintenance: An Inquiry Into Values* was first published by William Morrow in April 1974.

Stephanie Savage's statement about leaving behind more than one's own Facebook profile for subsequent generations was in the magazine *Self Service* (Spring/Summer 2010).

Slavoj Žižek wrote about *Titanic* and lots of other stuff on defaultgrey. blogspot.com, accessed on March 4th, 2010. Per Meland informed me about the entry when he heard of my book project. This particular article from *The New Statesman* can be found at http://www.newstatesman.com/film/2010/03/avatar-reality-love-couple-sex.

Frank O'Hara's poem 'Having a Coke with You' was taken from *The Collected Poems of Frank O'Hara*, Knopf (1971).

Fernando García-Dory, who spoke about happiness in 'A Shepherd's Life,' is also an artist. Among other things, he has published *A Shepherd's School As a Micro-kingdom of Utopia* (2010).

Both U.S. Ambassador to Norway, Barry White, and the director of the Norwegian Nobel Institute, Geir Lundestad, told me what Barack Obama exclaimed when he heard he'd won the Nobel Peace Prize.

Chapter 11. Canal Street, Manhattan: Shit!

E. B. White published *Here is New York* in 1949. It is the best book about the city I've ever read. The edition that I have is from The Little Bookroom (1999).

Orhan Pamuk's *The Museum of Innocence* was first published in English by Alfred A. Knopf in 2009, translated by Maureen Freely.

Astronaut Mike Mullane's quote about selling his wife and kids into slavery for a ride into space was taken from Mary Roach, *Packing for Mars*, W.W. Norton & Company (2010).

Chapter 13. Queens Storm Drain, Queens: The Past Lives On

The Great Gatsby by F. Scott Fitzgerald was first published in 1925 by Charles Scribner's Sons.

If there are quotes that I haven't cited, such as from Bart Simpson or from Socrates, it's because I don't remember where I got them from. For translations where no source is given, the quote has been translated by Erling Kagge or Becky L. Crook.

TRANSLATOR'S NOTE

The English translations of Dante throughout this book are from numerous sources. Though a translator usually chooses to use a single source, in this case I have decided to use multiple English translations depending on which were closest to the Norwegian translation of Dante that Erling Kagge used in his original manuscript. In some cases, I translated the lines of Dante myself, not because I believed my translation to be better than the experts, but because the lines rather better suited Kagge's Norwegian versions of Dante, and these meanings were often central to his arguments. The quotations of Dante throughout the book are therefore taken from the following translations, listed chronologically by date of their initial publication:

Translation by Henry Wadsworth Longfellow (1867):
Inferno, Canto V, line 120 ('There is no greater sorrow/Than to be mindful of the happy time/In misery.')
Inferno, Canto XXXIV, lines 135–139 ('And with no care for any rest, we climbed—/he first, I following—until I saw,/through a round opening, some of those things/of beauty Heaven bears. It was from there/that we emerged, to see—once more—the stars.')

Translation by John Ciardi (1977)
Inferno, Canto III, line 9 ('Abandon all hope, ye who enter here.')

Translation by Allen Mandelbaum (1980)
Inferno, Canto III, line 14 (The original translation uses the word 'hesitation' but the author here changed it to 'doubt.' ('Here one must leave behind all doubt; here every cowardice must meet its death')
Inferno, Canto IV, line 22 ('My ample theme impels me onward')

Purgatorio, Canto I, lines 58–60 and 70–72 ('This man had yet to see his final evening; but through his folly, little time was left before he did—he was so close to it. [...] He goes in search of liberty—so previous, as he who gives his life for it must know.')

Translation by James Finn Cotter, (2000)
Paradiso, Canto XXXIII, line 123 ('Oh how pale is language and how paltry/For [...] what I saw/My words are not enough.')

Translation by Robin Kirkpatrick (1996)
Inferno, Canto VI, line 87 ('But when you walk once more where life is sweet, bring me, I beg, to others in remembrance. No more I'll say, nor answer any more')
Inferno, Canto IX, line 74 ('"And now," he said, "stretch straight/Your strings of sight across this age-old scum/To where the fumes are thickest, stinging most."')

Translated freely by Becky L. Crook from the Norwegian translation of Dante used by Erling Kagge
Inferno, Canto V, line 38 ('Placing desire/and passion higher than reason')

THANKS

Thanks to Steve for friendship. Thanks to Gabi Gleichmann, Lars Fr. H. Svendsen, Michelle Andrews, Nick Baylis, Petter Skavlan, and Henrik M. Mestad, Anne Gaathaug (who does my job), Kristin Johansen, Therese Tungen, and everyone in Kagge Forlag for help with this book. Thanks also to Ingrid, Solveig, Nor, and Jorunn for allowing me to go, and to Alan, Jacki, Will, Brent, Andrew, and Liz for coming along.

For more information visit us at www.worldeditions.org.